# Contents

# Introduction

A feudal monarch like King Richard II might be the most powerful man in England, but he was not strong enough to govern without the country's formidable aristocratic establishment. These barons, or magnates, had sworn oaths of allegiance to the king but possessed considerable regional powers of their own. With insufficient wealth or military force under his own immediate control, a medieval king had inevitably to rely on these mighty lords for financial and military support.

The balance of power between an English medieval king and his nobles was inherently unstable. Peace and unity within the country depended on a strong and effective monarchy, but the more independent the king became the more uneasy were his nobles, who regarded it as their natural right to share in the government of the country. Richard realised this very early in life. Succeeding to the throne at the age of ten, he had for many years to endure being controlled by his uncle John of Gaunt, Duke of Lancaster.

As he grew older, Richard, with the support of younger nobles, took advantage of Gaunt's temporary absence from the country to exert greater personal control of the government of the country, a move which enraged many of the more senior magnates. In 1388, five powerful lords (called the Lords Appellant), led by another of Richard's uncles, the Duke of Gloucester, moved against the king and even threatened to depose him. When Richard attempted to resist, Gloucester allied with two of the other Lords Appellant, Henry Bullingbrook (or Bolingbroke, see page 119), Duke of Hereford, and Thomas Mowbray, Duke of Norfolk, and their combined forces defeated the king's army. Richard had to watch helplessly as his friends and supporters were accused, imprisoned and executed.

But Richard knew how to bide his time. While the Lords Appellant took over the reins of government, Richard quietly set about rebuilding his personal power and influence. To exalt the royal image, he created a flamboyantly dazzling court, built up his personal power bases in Ireland and Wales and expanded his own private standing army.

Richard waited for eight years. Then in 1397 he made his move. Three of the Lords Appellant were arrested. One was executed, one banished and the Duke of Gloucester died in prison in suspicious circumstances. In Parliament, a nervous House of Lords granted Richard powers greater than any English king had ever wielded before.

Some historical sources claim that just before Gloucester was arrested he had been plotting with Bullingbrook and Mowbray to carry out another political coup. The three intended to imprison Richard and his uncles, John of Gaunt and Edmund Duke of York, then put to death the rest of the King's Council. Mowbray, it is claimed, revealed this plot to Richard, who promptly arrested Gloucester and had him sent to Calais under Mowbray's charge, where he mysteriously died.

After Gloucester's death a very public quarrel broke out between the two remaining Lords Appellant. Bullingbrook accused Mowbray of treasonable talk, alleging amongst other things that Mowbray had murdered the Duke of Gloucester and claimed that Richard was now plotting to destroy the two of them as he had the other Lords Appellant. Mowbray denied the charges and the whole affair was referred to the Court of Chivalry for the king's judgement. Both men were put under arrest. Bullingbrook was released on bail under the charge of his father Gaunt, but Mowbray was detained in Windsor Castle. The two men must have feared for their lives.

This is where Shakespeare begins his story. What was King Richard hoping to achieve when he opened proceedings in the Court of Chivalry? Was he still out for revenge on the last two Lords Appellant? Or was Mowbray now a trusted supporter? If the king wanted revenge on Bullingbrook, he could not forget that he was a royal prince and cousin, son of Gaunt, the most powerful man in England after the king.

Why should Bullingbrook have made his allegations? Was it out of hatred of Mowbray for betraying the Lords Appellant or out of loyalty to the king? Was he indirectly attacking the king through one of his supporters, or trying to save his own skin by betraying Mowbray?

Given King Richard's seemingly secure political position at the start of the play, his downfall is remarkably sudden. In April 1398 he was supremely powerful. In September 1399 he was forced to resign the crown. By February 1400 he was dead. How could it have happened so quickly? Shakespeare's play gives a fascinating view of events that still had the power to shake the Elizabethan world almost 200 years later.

# Commentary

## Act 1 Scene 1

King Richard prepares to preside as judge in the Court of Chivalry, a special court of law formed to resolve disputes between men of high rank. Henry Bullingbrook (Bolingbroke), Duke of Hereford, has 'appealed' (accused) Thomas Mowbray, Duke of Norfolk, of high treason, to which Mowbray has laid a like counter-charge. Richard opens proceedings with the assured confidence of a man who expects to be obeyed:

> Old John of Gaunt, time-honoured Lancaster,
> Hast thou according to thy oath and band
> Brought hither Henry Herford, thy bold son,
> Here to make good the boisterous late appeal,
> Which then our leisure would not let us hear,
> Against the Duke of Norfolk, Thomas Mowbray?
>
> *(lines 1–6)*

When Gaunt confirms that his son is ready to make good his accusation, the king summons both 'appellants' into his presence. It is clear he expects it will be difficult to resolve this dispute. Both men are proud and arrogant ('High stomached'), their anger powerful as the elements themselves, 'deaf as the sea, hasty as fire'. Yet despite the seriousness of the occasion, as each man greets the king with glowing expressions of respect and loyalty, Richard cannot resist observing sardonically: 'We thank you both. Yet one but flatters us.'

First Bullingbrook formally states his accusation against Mowbray. For all its ringing words, his charge is quite simple. Mowbray is a traitor and he (Bullingbrook) stands ready to make good that accusation in Trial by Combat if necessary:

> With a foul traitor's name stuff I thy throat,
> And wish (so please my sovereign) ere I move,
> What my tongue speaks my right drawn sword may prove.
>
> *(lines 44–6)*

Mowbray's answer is equally direct. He calls Bullingbrook 'a slanderous coward and a villain' and says that, if permitted to ignore Bullingbrook's royal blood, he would be more than willing to prove his loyalty to the king in single combat at any place Bullingbrook might care to choose. Unhesitatingly, Bullingbrook sets aside the protection of his royal connections and throws down his 'gage' (gauntlet) to challenge Mowbray to Trial by Combat. Equally promptly, Mowbray takes up Bullingbrook's gage to accept the challenge.

The manner in which this trial is conducted would have seemed distinctly archaic even to an Elizabethan audience, for this is the legal process of the late Middle Ages, a feudal society where the concepts of loyalty and personal honour are supremely important. Instead of modern legal 'proof' (evidence, witnesses, statements) there is only the word of a man of honour. An accusation of high treason (the term for activities that threatened the security of the state or the king himself), if denied, could have only one outcome: a challenge to personal combat. God would be deemed to have ensured that truth prevailed by granting victory to the right man.

King Richard, however, requires Bullingbrook to make his accusations more specific. So Bullingbrook lists three charges: (1) Mowbray kept money from the king intended to pay the king's army, (2) he has been responsible for all the treasons hatched in England for the past 18 years and (3) he played a major part in the murder of the Duke of Gloucester.

As Bullingbrook makes his third accusation, his words take on an added power and resonance, for this crime strikes to the heart of the royal family. Gloucester was uncle to both Richard and Bullingbrook, brother to Richard's father, the legendary Black Prince, and son of King Edward III. Using images of blood and cries for vengeance, Bullingbrook describes how Mowbray:

> like a traitor coward
> Sluiced out his [Gloucester's] innocent soul through streams of
>    blood,
> Which blood, like sacrificing Abel's, cries
> Even from the tongueless caverns of the earth
> To me for justice and rough chastisement          *(lines 102–6)*

The question of who murdered the Duke of Gloucester will play a significant part in the opening scenes of the play. Many Elizabethans would have known that Richard himself was strongly suspected of ordering Mowbray to kill his uncle. Bullingbrook perhaps even dares to hint as much in his reference to 'sacrificing Abel' (in the Bible, Abel was killed by his brother Cain). It is easy therefore to imagine an edge to Richard's amused response to Bullingbrook's passionate outburst: 'How high a pitch his resolution soars!'

Perhaps Richard suspects that Bullingbrook, though ostensibly accusing Mowbray, is challenging the crown itself. The king may insist that Bullingbrook is not his 'kingdom's heir' and merely his 'father's brother's son' (lines 116–17), but as Richard was childless his royal cousin would indeed be very close in succession to the throne.

What must surely make Richard very uneasy is that if he *had* ordered Gloucester's murder it is vital that Mowbray now remains silent on the matter. So with a show of scrupulous impartiality, he assures Mowbray that Bullingbrook's royal connections will in no way influence his judgement:

> He is our subject, Mowbray; so art thou.
> Free speech and fearless I to thee allow.          *(lines 122–3)*

In his defence, Mowbray quickly deals with the accusation of embezzling the king's money, but on the matter of Gloucester's murder his answer is more ambiguous. He denies murdering Gloucester but regrets he 'Neglected [his] sworn duty in that case' (line 134). Mowbray then gives a blanket denial to Bullingbrook's allegation that he had been the source of all the treasonous plots for the past 18 years, although he does admit to once attempting to kill John of Gaunt, a crime he has already confessed to. At which point, he too throws down his gage to counter-challenge Bullingbrook to Trial by Combat.

The dispute now comes to a head. As judge and arbiter, Richard, with Gaunt's help, attempts to reconcile the two fiery dukes. But since the ancient code of chivalry gave Bullingbrook the right to challenge his uncle's murderer to combat, Richard cannot command him to withdraw, only grant or deny his request. To emphasise that this trial is therefore as much a contest of strength between the king and his nobles as it is between Bullingbrook and Mowbray, the 1980 Royal Shakespeare Company production showed Richard being forced to descend from his throne to physically prevent Bullingbrook from picking up Mowbray's gage (at line 150). The king and Gaunt then attempt without success to persuade the two appellants to throw down the other's gage. Both refuse.

Again the king commands Mowbray to throw down Bullingbrook's gage. But Mowbray passionately defends his right to fight. Repeatedly he speaks of 'honour', his 'fair name' and 'spotless reputation', of his 'shame' and 'dark dishonour' were he to back down now (lines 165–9 and 175–85). For the first time in the play, Richard gives Bullingbrook a direct command: 'Cousin, throw up your gage. Do you begin' (line 186). The future King Henry IV's answer is unequivocal. Rather than let his tongue 'sound so base a parle' (utter such an ignoble call for truce) he would rather tear out the offending organ with his teeth and 'spit it bleeding' in Mowbray's face. This is the final 'blood' image in an opening scene that is full of such images.

Having failed in his attempts at reconciliation, Richard grants the two dukes their Trial by Combat 'At Coventry upon Saint Lambert's Day'. Is this the action of a king unable to control his unruly nobles or is Richard privately content to see the dispute unresolved for the moment? Shakespeare leaves the question open for the audience to reflect on.

## Act 1 Scene 2

After the spectacular public confrontation in the opening scene, the audience now witnesses a private and intimate meeting between Gaunt and his widowed sister, the Duchess of Gloucester. If the audience were as yet unaware that the king himself might have been implicated in the Duke of Gloucester's death, Shakespeare makes it clear in this scene that both Gaunt and his sister-in-law are convinced he was.

Yet Gaunt refuses to be moved by the Duchess's pleas to avenge his brother's murder. The dilemma Gaunt faces is one that many others in the play will have to confront. What is a subject to do if the king, who should be the source of all justice and good government, fails in his responsibilities? Gaunt's solution is patient acceptance of the king's authority. Since only God has power to judge the actions of a king, 'Put we our quarrel to the will of heaven'.

This the Duchess refuses to accept. As she grieves for her dead husband, she uses images of cracked vials of King Edward III's 'sacred blood' and severed branches 'of his most royal root', to impress on

Gaunt the terrible damage that Richard's crime has done to the once flourishing Plantagenet dynasty. If Gaunt accepts his brother's murder, she argues, then Gaunt will surely be the next to die. His 'patience' is nothing but 'pale cold cowardice in noble breasts'. The best way for Gaunt to safeguard his own life is to avenge his brother's murder. Yet still Gaunt refuses. Richard is 'God's substitute, / His deputy' on earth 'anointed in His sight' and Gaunt will 'never lift / An angry arm against His minister' (lines 37–8 and 40–1). The Duchess must look to God for justice and redress.

Brother and sister-in-law take leave of each other. Gaunt is to go to Coventry to witness his son's Trial by Combat, the Duchess to her home in Plashy. Grief has almost broken her mind. She bids Gaunt commend her to his brother Edmund Duke of York, but then changes her mind and asks him to bid York visit her at Plashy, then changes her mind again. Her final words make it clear that she and Gaunt will never see each other alive again:

> Desolate, desolate will I hence and die.
> The last leave of thee takes my weeping eye.    *(lines 73–4)*

## Act 1 Scene 3

The actual Trial by Combat between Bullingbrook and Mowbray was a dazzlingly magnificent event as the aristocracy of England gathered to watch two of England's most famous knights in a savage fight to the death. Even if the loser were still alive at the end of the contest the rules required that he be dragged from the lists (combat area) to be hanged or beheaded.

Shakespeare builds up the tension and pageantry stage by ceremonial stage. First the Lord Marshal checks that both combatants are ready, then the trumpets sound to announce the entry of King Richard and his nobles to witness the battle. The king commands the Lord Marshal to demand of each combatant his name and why he comes to fight, after which the Lord Marshal declares that no one 'on pain of death' is to interfere with the battle other than himself and his appointed officers.

Next come the ritual leave-takings. Bullingbrook bids farewell first to his king, then to his other cousin, Lord Aumerle, and finally to his father Gaunt. Richard may appear to do his cousin an honour by coming down from his ceremonial seat to embrace him, but his perfunctory words of support have an equivocal ring should the audience believe that the king himself has a personal interest in the outcome of the battle:

> Cousin of Herford, as thy cause is right
> So be thy fortune in this royal fight. *(lines 55–6)*

Gaunt argued in the previous scene that avenging the death of Gloucester should be left to the will of God, but when Bullingbrook asks his father's blessing to help him revive the glory of the family name, Gaunt is wholehearted in his son's support. His ties of blood are clearly stronger than his sense of duty to the king:

> And let thy blows, doubly redoubled,
> Fall like amazing thunder on the casque
> Of thy adverse pernicious enemy. *(lines 80–2)*

Mowbray makes his farewells with declarations of his own honesty, loyalty to the king and eagerness for the coming battle. If Mowbray had murdered Gloucester on instructions from the king, what feelings does Richard have for him now? His somewhat perfunctory farewell to Mowbray reveals little:

> Farewell, my lord. Securely I espy
> Virtue with valour couchèd in thine eye.
> Order the trial, Marshal, and begin. *(lines 97–9)*

The tension mounts. Both combatants receive their lances, their heralds issue final challenges and the Lord Marshal orders the trumpets to sound the charge. At which point King Richard suddenly throws down his 'warder' (ceremonial staff) to bring the battle to a halt. Historical records state how the king's last-minute intervention created a veritable sensation.

Giving for the moment no explanation for his actions, the king tells the combatants to disarm and return to their former positions, orders the members of the King's Council to withdraw with him and commands the trumpets to sound until his return. There is a short pause as he consults with his Privy Council (the actual meeting lasted for two hours while the combatants waited in their tents).

A feudal king was quite within his rights to halt the Trial by Combat at any time, but many have been puzzled as to what motive Shakespeare's Richard might have for leaving it so dramatically late. Is it born out of panic and guilt or, as Graham Holderness argues (see pages 95–6), a 'deliberate, carefully planned and decisive intervention', a very public demonstration of the king's power over his nobility's militaristic feudal customs? This second view is very much endorsed by the confident and measured manner of Richard's subsequent words to the assembled nobles (lines 123–43). Emphasising that his decision has been taken with the full agreement of his council of nobles (which included Gaunt), he declares that both combatants are to be banished so that England may be protected from the threat of civil war sparked off by 'the eagle-wingèd pride' of over-powerful warring lords.

Banishing both men could indeed be regarded as a skilful piece of political manoeuvring. At one stroke Richard gets rid of a powerful threat to his throne and a potential blackmailer. Perhaps more significantly, he has now dealt with the two remaining Lords Appellant who had so humiliated him eight years previously (see page 4).

Bullingbrook's response to being banished for ten years is dignified but defiant:

> Your will be done. This must my comfort be:
> That sun that warms you here shall shine on me    *(lines 144–5)*

Mowbray, however, is banished for life. His words are equally dignified but he cannot conceal the pain he feels that his loyal service should be so harshly rewarded:

> A heavy sentence, my most sovereign liege,
> And all unlooked for from your highness' mouth.    *(lines 154–5)*

For Mowbray the greatest pain of banishment will be to no longer speak his native language. He talks movingly of how his tongue will be like 'an unstringèd viol or a harp' imprisoned in his mouth for ever. But Richard is unmoved and almost callous in his response:

> It boots thee not to be compassionate.
> After our sentence plaining [complaining] comes too late.
>
> *(lines 174–5)*

Finally, both Mowbray and Bullingbrook are forced to swear an oath never to conspire together against the king (the historical Richard made great use of oaths to enforce loyalty to the crown). Before Mowbray departs into banishment, Bullingbrook issues one final challenge for him to confess his guilt. In reply, Mowbray claims to know what Bullingbrook is really like rather than what he appears to be. The significance of his words will echo through the play:

> But what thou art, God, thou and I do know,
> And all too soon, I fear, the king shall rue.　　　*(lines 203–4)*

Then suddenly Richard reduces Bullingbrook's period of banishment by four years, giving as his reason Gaunt's distress at his son's term of banishment. Whether the king's concern is genuine or a show of leniency to placate the most powerful noble in the land, the audience cannot yet be sure. Bullingbrook, however, reacts with sardonic amusement, reflecting, like his erstwhile opponent Mowbray, on the power and importance of language:

> How long a time lies in one little word.
> Four lagging winters and four wanton springs
> End in a word, such is the breath of kings.　　　*(lines 212–14)*

For Gaunt, however, even six years will be too long. One of the last two ageing sons of Edward III, he knows he is close to death and will never live to see his son again. When Richard reminds him that he was party to his son's sentence, Gaunt politely reproaches him. Gaunt did not want to be seen to be partial in his judgement of his son and had hoped that the king would have shown leniency on his behalf. Richard's response is again uncompromising: 'Six years we banish him and he shall go.'

With the departure of the king and his court, father and son are left alone to say their farewells. Bullingbrook is initially silent. Gaunt tries to make him see his situation in a positive light, but Bullingbrook will not be persuaded. In their shared sorrow, the conversation increasingly comes to resemble a philosophical debate on the nature of language, thought and reality. Gaunt argues that Bullingbrook's mind has power to create the reality it desires:

Think not the king did banish thee,
But thou the king.                                          *(lines 278–9)*

Look what thy soul holds dear, imagine it
To lie that way thou goest, not whence thou com'st.
                                                            *(lines 285–6)*

Bullingbrook, however, cannot accept that imagination, through language, has any power to change reality:

Oh, who can hold a fire in his hand
By thinking on the frosty Caucasus?
Or cloy the hungry edge of appetite
By bare imagination of a feast?                            *(lines 293–6)*

Gaunt leaves with his son to see him on his way to exile. Their strangely philosophical debate may now be ended but the questions it has raised about language and reality will be explored further as the play presents the twin stories of King Richard and the future King Henry IV.

## Act 1 Scene 4

So far, the audience has seen only the public face of Richard in his role as impartial monarch. Now we see him in intimate conversation with his trusted advisers, and his sarcastic reference to 'high Herford' reveals immediately that the formal respect shown to his cousin in public was all a sham. The king and Lord Aumerle clearly both despise and fear Bullingbrook. Richard talks scornfully of his popularity with the common people and how he behaved as if he had ambitions for the crown itself:

Off goes his bonnet to an oysterwench.
A brace of draymen bid God speed him well
And had the tribute of his supple knee,
With 'Thanks, my countrymen, my loving friends',
As were our England in reversion his,
And he our subjects' next degree in hope.                  *(lines 31–6)*

When one of the king's personal advisers, Sir Henry Green, brings up affairs of state, the audience also begins to see the financial problems that Richard's policies have created. A rebellion in Ireland urgently needs quelling. Richard intends to conduct the war himself. But wars and personal armies cost money. We learn (lines 42–52) that the high cost of maintaining his court together with the king's 'liberal largesse' (giving of grants to selected people to secure their loyalty) means that the country must now be 'farmed'. Here, parts of the country are allocated to 'tax-farmers', who pay the king money for the right to extort taxes on their own behalf. If that proves not to be sufficient, Richard plans to give his deputies left in England powers to use 'blank charters'. This was the practice of making rich individuals who had given support (real or imagined) to the king's enemies sign blank documents promising donations to the crown, which the king could fill in later with whatever amount he chose.

At this point comes news that Gaunt is 'grievous sick'. The John of Gaunt of the play has been a loyal and faithful servant to the king, but Richard's reaction to the sad news is shockingly callous. If Gaunt dies, he can confiscate his lands and money to help finance his war in Ireland:

> Now put it, God, in the physician's mind
> To help him to his grave immediately.
> The lining of his coffers shall make coats
> To deck our soldiers for these Irish wars.
> Come, gentlemen, let's all go visit him.
> Pray God we may make haste and come too late.     *(lines 58–63)*

Richard, however, is not merely forfeiting the audience's sympathy at this moment by his monstrous lack of feeling. More ominously, he is embarking on a course of action that will have tragic consequences for himself and his country for generations to come.

## Act 1 Critical review

In the struggle for ascendancy between king and nobles, Richard appears to be supreme. Gaunt, the most powerful man in England after the king, is dying and Bullingbrook, his son and heir, is banished. Permanently exiling Mowbray has reduced the risk of any revelation of the king's involvement in Gloucester's murder.

Richard's aura of authority is given visible expression through ceremonial demonstrations of respect in the public scenes, where the dominant stage image is of the king set high on his throne with Gaunt by his side. As counterpoint to these public scenes of ritual and pageantry, Shakespeare places two quiet and intimate moments: Gaunt's painful conversation with Gloucester's grieving widow; and Richard's private meeting with his favourites, the close friends and advisers with whose support he really governs England.

The two 'private' scenes reveal that even close members of the royal family believe Richard ordered his uncle Gloucester's death, an action that has struck at the heart of the ruling dynasty. Both Bullingbrook and Gloucester's widow desire revenge and only respect for Richard's divine right to rule prevents Gaunt from joining them. Richard is clearly nervous of Bullingbrook's popularity with the people, no doubt prompting his decision to banish him.

Bullingbrook presents himself as a man of action, a champion of justice, seeker of the truth and a 'true born Englishman', but his real intentions are unclear. His courting of the common people suggests he may harbour political ambitions, and while he claims to accuse Mowbray out of loyal concern for 'the precious safety' of the king, his actions can also be seen as an indirect attack on Richard.

Richard's England, with its pageantry and militaristic code of chivalry, is a medieval world at the point of change. The heroic age of Edward III has almost passed away. Five of the legendary king's sons are dead, a sixth (Gaunt) is dying and the struggle for power between two of their descendants, Richard and Bullingbrook, is about to begin. This sense of an imminent seismic change is reflected in the opening act's many elemental images of earth, air, fire and water, and of rising and falling. Also prominent are images of blood, with its connotations of kinship, murder and war.

# Act 2 Scene 1

The dying Gaunt hopes fervently the king will visit him so he can spend his final moments giving 'wholesome counsel to his unstaid [wild, uncontrolled] youth'. Gaunt's brother, Edmund Duke of York, advises him to save his breath: 'For all in vain comes counsel to his ear' (line 4). Gaunt, however, refuses to believe that the king will not listen to his death-bed counsel. His words are a strangely moving mixture of music and pain:

> Oh, but they say the tongues of dying men
> Enforce attention like deep harmony.
> Where words are scarce they are seldom spent in vain,
> For they breathe truth that breathe their words in pain.
>
> *(lines 5–8)*

York remains unconvinced. Richard is young, too easily led by flatterers, too fond of following foreign fashions, too rashly determined to go his own way (lines 17–30). Provoked by his brother's pessimism, Gaunt launches into a passionate lament for the sorry state into which his country has degenerated.

Gaunt's thoughts unfold, as they often do in Shakespeare's longer speeches, in three stages. First, like 'a prophet new inspired' he looks into the future (lines 31–9). Richard's extravagant and irresponsible lifestyle, 'His rash fierce blaze of riot', is unsustainable (an accurate prophecy). Then (lines 40–58) he looks to the past. Line by line, and phrase by phrase, he conjures up a vision of the England he once knew, the gloriously proud world of King Edward III and the Black Prince, King Richard's father. This England was truly great and happy, a 'precious stone set in the silver sea', peopled by a 'happy breed of men', whose 'royal kings' were feared and famous as far abroad as Jerusalem itself. Finally he gives vent to his anger at how, under Richard's misguided rule, his beloved England has been engulfed in financial corruption:

> This land of such dear souls, this dear, dear land,
> Dear for her reputation through the world,
> Is now leased out, I die pronouncing it,
> Like to a tenement or pelting farm     *(lines 57–60)*

With mounting passion, he condemns the policies that have brought about his country's disintegration. England was once 'bound in' [bordered] only by 'the triumphant sea', but now is 'bound in' in another sense (i.e. legally bonded, leased out):

> bound in with shame,
> With inky blots and rotten parchment bonds,
> That England that was wont to conquer others
> Hath made a shameful conquest of itself      *(lines 63–6)*

When the king arrives with his queen and the rest of the court, Gaunt does not hesitate to criticise him to his face. In answer to Richard's enquiry about his health, Gaunt (lines 73–83) plays bitterly with his own name, saying that he has become 'gaunt' through constant watching over 'sleeping England' and grieving for his banished son:

> Gaunt am I for the grave, gaunt as a grave,
> Whose hollow womb inherits naught but bones.    *(lines 82–3)*

He may be dying, Gaunt says, but it is the king who is the sicker man. England is Richard's 'deathbed', his reputation is 'sick' and he is entrusting his cure to the very 'physicians' who first made him ill, the 'thousand flatterers' who 'sit within [his] crown' (lines 91–103). If King Edward III had known how foolishly his grandson would dissipate his great inheritance, he would have excluded him from the succession:

> Landlord of England art thou now, not king,
> Thy state of law is bondslave to the law     *(lines 113–14)*

These accusations are too much for Richard to bear. Pale with fury, the king warns Gaunt that only his close kinship to King Edward protects him from losing his head. But Gaunt will not be restrained and openly accuses the king of Gloucester's murder. Reluctance to spill the blood of King Edward's son, Gaunt claims, did not prevent his brother Gloucester's death. The king 'like the pelican' (a bird believed to wound its own breast to feed its young) has already 'drunkenly caroused' on his own uncle's blood. Gaunt orders his servants to carry him from the king's presence. He no longer wishes to live in a world without love and honour.

York attempts to excuse his brother's behaviour (lines 143–6), insisting that Gaunt loves Richard as much as his own son, but the king clearly harbours such a long-standing hostility towards both Gaunt and his son that when Northumberland enters with news that Gaunt has died, Richard does not even bother to make a show of grief:

> The ripest fruit first falls, and so doth he.
> His time is spent, our pilgrimage must be.
> So much for that. *(lines 153–5)*

After this contemptuous dismissal, Richard announces his decision to confiscate Gaunt's property to help finance his Irish wars. English kings had confiscated lands and property before. Richard himself had appropriated the Duke of Gloucester's possessions and seizure of Gaunt's vast Lancastrian estates would greatly ease the king's financial difficulties while simultaneously removing a powerful rival in Gaunt's son, Bullingbrook.

Such a move was, however, extremely risky. It was an act of tyranny, putting the king's will above the law, as York is about to point out. All his life Richard has been lectured to by uncles: first Gaunt and Gloucester and now York! In one production, when Richard announced his intention to seize Gaunt's property (lines 159–62), the king placed his hands over his ears in expectation of the outburst he knew was going to come.

York is reproachful. Never before has he wavered in his allegiance to the king, despite many provocations – Gloucester's death, Bullingbrook's banishment, the rebuking of Gaunt, his own disgrace – but now he must protest. Richard's father (the Black Prince), he says, directed his anger at the French, not his own people; he spent only what he won in battle and did not waste the wealth his father had acquired; his hands were red only with the blood of enemies not his kinsmen. It is all too much for the grief-stricken York (lines 184–5).

When Richard pretends not to understand York's distress, the old man makes his concerns unequivocally clear (lines 186–208). The illegal seizure of Gaunt's 'royalties and rights', which now belong to Bullingbrook, strikes at the heart of the feudal contract, which demanded respect for law and tradition from both king and lord. If

Bullingbrook cannot claim his inheritance, then neither can the king claim his. The balanced patterns of York's questions almost physically express this mutuality:

> Is not Gaunt dead? And doth not Herford live?
> Was not Gaunt just? And is not Harry true?
> Did not the one deserve to have an heir?
> Is not his heir a well-deserving son?
> Take Herford's rights away and take from time
> His charters and his customary rights.
> Let not tomorrow then ensue today.
> Be not thyself. For how art thou a king
> But by fair sequence and succession? *(lines 191–9)*

York's prophecy (like Gaunt's in lines 31–9) is grim. If Richard disinherits Bullingbrook, he risks losing the allegiance of the entire aristocratic establishment (lines 200–8). Richard does not even pause to reconsider, seemingly confident in his power to do exactly as he wishes. So York leaves, unwilling to be witness to an act which can have only disastrous consequences. Richard immediately organises the confiscation of Gaunt's lands and revenues and decides to leave for Ireland the next day, naming York as his deputy in his absence. Is it wise to leave the country when his barons are so obviously unhappy? Is it sensible to leave York in charge considering his recent angry haranguing of the king? Richard seems to find a certain ironic pleasure in doing so:

> And we create in absence of ourself
> Our uncle York lord governor of England,
> For he is just, and always loved us well. *(lines 219–21)*

When Richard departs with his queen and his supporters, the Earl of Northumberland and two other lords remain behind. All three are clearly unhappy about the king's actions, but reluctant to voice their concerns openly for fear of being accused of treason until Northumberland encourages them to be frank (lines 230–1).

Ross and Willoughby, as York had prophesied, are angry at Bullingbrook's loss of his inheritance, fearing no doubt that they will be next to suffer. Northumberland fears the machinations of the king's advisers, who will do all they can to provoke the king to 'severely prosecute / 'Gainst us, our lives, our children and our heirs' (lines 244–5). As the three men's trust in each other grows (lines 246–61), so their criticisms become more outspoken, echoing the complaints already made by Gaunt and York. Richard has bled the House of Commons with heavy taxes, fined the nobility, extracted money using 'blanks' and 'benevolences' and put 'the realm in farm' (see page 15). Rather than wage honourable wars abroad, he has 'basely' given up foreign territory won by his ancestors. Indeed, he has spent more in peacetime than his ancestors ever did in war.

Northumberland now judges the time is right for action. Although the storm is about to sink their ship, he says, they 'strike not' (meaning 'do not take in the sails' but also hinting at taking up arms). However, he has news of Bullingbrook that may give them hope:

> Even through the hollow eyes of death
> I spy life peering, but I dare not say
> How near the tidings of our comfort is.            *(lines 270–2)*

Bullingbrook is making his way back to England with an army of supporters. The leading figures that Northumberland lists in Bullingbrook's force reveal the depth of resentment building against Richard (lines 277–85). There is, for example, the son of the Earl of Arundel, the Lord Appellant executed for treason by Richard in 1397, and the earl's brother, removed from his post as Archbishop of Canterbury for the same reason. The factions opposed to Richard are clearly uniting in support of Bullingbrook.

What Northumberland's stirring account cannot entirely hide, however, is that Bullingbrook's force is tiny – just eight ships and 3,000 men at arms (line 286). Nevertheless, Ross and Willoughby respond unhesitatingly to Northumberland's call to go with him to join Bullingbrook at Ravenspurgh and race each other to get to Bullingbrook first (lines 299–300).

The historical events represented in this one scene in fact extended over several months. By compressing them together, Shakespeare has dramatically created a sense of the swift inexorable progress of history, which Richard is powerless to halt, so that almost before the king has left for Ireland the forces that will ultimately overthrow him seem to be gathering against him.

## Act 2 Scene 2

In Scene 1, Northumberland and the other disaffected lords watched the departure of a callous tyrant and 'degenerate king'. In this next scene Shakespeare presents the king in a different light. His queen clearly grieves at being parted from her 'sweet Richard' and her mind is filled with a premonition of impending disaster:

> Some unborn sorrow ripe in Fortune's womb
> Is coming towards me, and my inward soul
> With nothing trembles                    *(lines 10–12)*

Many critics see the play as full of shifting and contradictory viewpoints or 'perspectives' like this. Events are constantly seen from multiple points of view. So far Shakespeare has allowed Mowbray, Bullingbrook, Gaunt, York, Northumberland, and now the queen to present their particular view of events and there will be other focuses for the audience's sympathy (notably Richard himself) in the later acts.

Shakespeare seems to signal the existence of multiple viewpoints in the speech he gives to Bushy, one of the king's advisers (lines 14–27). In an attempt to comfort the queen, Bushy makes use of two strangely shifting similes: the perspective glass and the perspective picture (see explanation on pages 67–8). At one moment (lines 14–17) he seems to say that the queen's tears have blurred ('glazèd') the image of the world she sees, as if she were looking through a perspective glass, so that her genuine sorrow is multiplied into 'twenty shadows'. Then the next moment (lines 18–20) he seems to say that she sees imaginary fears because she does not look 'rightly' at the world, just as people see hidden images ('Distinguish form') when they look 'awry' at a perspective picture. The queen, therefore, must look her sorrow squarely in the face and see it for what it really is – just a temporary parting from her husband:

> Then, thrice-gracious queen,
> More than your lord's departure weep not. More's not seen,
> Or if it be 'tis with false sorrow's eye
> Which for things true weeps things imaginary.    *(lines 24–7)*

It is an elegant attempt at comforting the queen (in one production Bagot and the ladies-in-waiting applauded at the end of Bushy's speech) but it fails to allay her fears. Her sorrow is not 'conceit' (imagination, thinking), she says, because an imaginary sorrow will always have an underlying cause, while her sorrow seems born out of nothing at all. The tangles in her syntax match the confusion in her thoughts:

> But what it is that is not yet known what
> I cannot name; 'tis nameless woe I wot [think].     *(lines 39–40)*

The queen's fears are proved valid almost immediately. Green, another of the king's advisers, brings news that Bullingbrook has landed with an army in Yorkshire, where Northumberland and many other northern lords have joined him. The Earl of Worcester (Northumberland's brother and Richard's steward) has also defected to Bullingbrook, along with the king's entire royal household. The whole of England is at the mercy of the rebels. The queen now knows the source of her 'nameless woe'. It is Bullingbrook (lines 62–6).

York, Richard's deputy Protector of England, enters. The difficult task of organising the defence of the kingdom is clearly beyond him, as he himself acknowledges (lines 80–5), and his distress is only intensified by news that his son, the Duke of Aumerle, has disappeared and his sister-in-law, the Duchess of Gloucester, has died. More significantly, he has deeply divided family loyalties. He owes allegiance both to his nephew the King and to the nephew that the king has disinherited:

> Both are my kinsmen.
> T'one is my sovereign, whom both my oath
> And duty bids defend; t'other again
> Is my kinsman, whom the king hath wronged,
> Whom conscience and my kindred bids to right.     *(lines 111–15)*

York orders those present to muster as many men as they can and meet him as soon as possible at Berkeley Castle in Gloucestershire. Then he leaves with the queen to find her a safe haven. There is not even time to go to Plashy for his sister-in-law's funeral.

Bushy, Green and Bagot are left alone to consider their fate. As Richard's favourites and close advisers, their 'nearness to the king in love' will make them the first to feel the rebels' anger, particularly 'the wavering commons' (House of Commons) who have been hardest hit by Richard's money-raising policies. Unfavourable winds are also preventing the return of Richard's army from Ireland so that the rebel forces easily outnumber the king's supporters left in England.

Bushy and Green plan to take refuge in Bristow (Bristol) castle, with the Earl of Wiltshire, another of the king's supporters. Bagot decides to join the king in Ireland. As they make their farewells, the three clearly believe they will never meet again. Their only hope of survival is for the Duke of York to hold out against Bullingbrook's rapidly increasing power, a manifestly impossible challenge, like 'numbering sands and drinking oceans dry' (line 144).

## Act 2 Scene 3

Shakespeare now switches the play's perspective from Richard's frightened and confused supporters to Bullingbrook and the powerful lords flocking to his side. Bullingbrook, accompanied by Northumberland, has moved swiftly from north-east England to the south west and is close to Berkeley Castle where York has taken up a defensive position with what remains of the king's supporters.

When Bullingbrook asks Northumberland how much farther they have to go, the earl, who had earlier spoken so contemptuously of Richard's flatterers (Act 2 Scene 1, lines 241–5), now shows he can more than match them in obsequiousness as he praises his companion's sweet 'as sugar' conversation (lines 2–7). Northumberland clearly sees where the future lies and is determined to be part of it.

Their conversation is interrupted by Northumberland's son, young Harry Percy, who brings news that Northumberland's brother, the Earl of Worcester, has resigned from the king's service and dismissed the royal household (a significant act because the royal household ran the king's administrative system). Bullingbrook accepts Harry Percy's offer of allegiance, thanks him warmly and promises to reward him when he can.

The murder of Gloucester and the golden age of Edward III have cast a long shadow over the play so far. Here Shakespeare sets up a situation to prompt his audience to look into the future. Many Elizabethans would have known that Bullingbrook's new allies (Northumberland, Percy and Worcester) will lead a rebellion against him some years later, events which Shakespeare dramatised in *King Henry IV Parts 1 and 2*. One production hinted here at their future falling-out by having Harry Percy burst in and push Bullingbrook aside as he sat down to rest.

Ross and Willoughby also arrive to offer their support. Again Bullingbrook thanks them and promises to reward them when his 'infant fortune comes to years' (line 66). These are politically charged moments. Each offer or acceptance of support, each handshake, embrace or kneeling, every word or gesture is crucial. Many critics believe that Shakespeare deliberately echoes amongst these Gloucestershire hills the formal rituals of allegiance shown to Richard in the play's opening scenes. One production had Northumberland bring his son to face Bullingbrook (line 40) and push him to his knees as a gesture of respect. Whereupon Bullingbrook also knelt, grasped Percy's hand, lifted him to his feet, embraced him and shook his hand again. In this way the audience was made aware, both visually and symbolically, of a significant shift in power.

Lord Berkeley arrives with a message from York, Governor of England, demanding to know why his nephew has returned from banishment to 'fright our native peace with self-born arms' (line 80). Bullingbrook knows he must assure York that his actions pose no threat to the king's authority. Indeed, some critics have questioned whether Shakespeare's Bullingbrook has any such intention – yet. He certainly makes it clear to Berkeley that he only comes to claim his rightful title of Duke of Lancaster. Before he can say more, York himself arrives. Again there is a show of ceremony as Bullingbrook kneels to his uncle, an action which angers York who believes it is a show of false humility (lines 83–4).

Before Bullingbrook can explain himself, York launches into an angry tirade. His nephew is a traitor who has returned before his time of banishment is up, bearing arms against 'the anointed king'. That these words are empty bluster, York himself seems to concede (lines 98–104) when he declares how he would have crushed Bullingbrook already were he not so old and stricken with 'the palsy' (shaking sickness).

In answering his uncle's charges (lines 112–35), Bullingbrook chooses his words with care. If York can be persuaded to side with him, Richard is surely doomed. Again Bullingbrook makes no reference to seeking any more than what is rightfully his. When he was banished it was as Duke of Hereford. But he returns as Duke of Lancaster (lines 112–13). Next Bullingbrook plays on family loyalty. With Gaunt dead, York has become his virtual father and no father would allow his son to be stripped of his birthright:

> Oh then, my father,
> Will you permit that I shall stand condemned
> A wandering vagabond, my rights and royalties
> Plucked from my arms perforce and given away
> To upstart unthrifts?                    *(lines 117–21)*

Then Bullingbrook advances an argument which cannot but move his uncle for it is the self-same warning that York had given Richard (Act 2 Scene 1, lines 195–208). By seizing Gaunt's lands, the king has broken the laws of inheritance, an act which strikes at the heart of the feudal contract and challenges even the king's own right to rule:

> If that my cousin king be king in England
> It must be granted I am Duke of Lancaster.    *(lines 122–3)*

Again Bullingbrook appeals to family loyalty (one production had him put his arm round his uncle's shoulder). If York had died and his son been thus treated, Gaunt would certainly have safeguarded Aumerle's inheritance. Bullingbrook has 'letters patents' (legal documents) to prove his claim and demands his inheritance 'of free descent' (by legal right), cleverly using his lack of legal representation as the reason for his return (lines 132–5).

Northumberland, Ross and Willoughby join in pleading Bullingbrook's cause. York wavers. He has sympathy for his nephew's claim, but still condemns the taking up of arms against the king, for that is rebellion (lines 139–46). When Northumberland insists that Bullingbrook has sworn on oath he comes 'But for his own' (line 148), York concedes. Since he cannot compel Bullingbrook to accept 'the sovereign mercy of the king', he will 'remain as neuter' (neutral).

Bullingbrook, however, wants more than mere neutrality. He politely pressures York to be more supportive of his cause, asking him to accompany them to Bristol Castle to deal with Bushy and Bagot, those 'caterpillars of the commonwealth' that Bullingbrook has 'sworn to weed and pluck away'. One production showed this pressure on

York by making him start to leave at line 158 ('So fare you well') only to find his way blocked by a silent Bullingbrook. York attempted to leave again at line 160 after inviting Bullingbrook to stay at Berkeley Castle for the night but again found his way blocked by his nephew. York's despairing indecision can be clearly felt in the to-and-fro movement of his final words:

> It may be I will go with you, but yet I'll pause,
> For I am loath to break our country's laws.
> Nor friends nor foes to me welcome you are.
> Things past redress are now with me past care.
>
> *(lines 167–70)*

## Act 2 Scene 4

Richard's one remaining hope of survival lies with his Welsh supporters. They have for days been expecting the king's return from Ireland, but will wait no longer. One of the Welsh captains informs the Earl of Salisbury that their army is going to disperse. Salisbury begs them to stay just one more day, but the Captain (a kind of representative of all of Richard's disheartened and dispirited followers) refuses. Omens have been seen in the heavens which foretell 'the death or fall of kings' (line 15).

Even Salisbury, the king's faithful supporter, believes the king's cause is lost. His final speech echoes the captain's cosmic imagery as he describes Richard's glory falling 'like a shooting star' and his sun setting 'weeping in the lowly west'. Heaven itself seems to have turned against his beloved king:

> Ah, Richard! With the eyes of heavy mind
> I see thy glory like a shooting star
> Fall to the base earth from the firmament.
> Thy sun sets weeping in the lowly west,
> Witnessing storms to come, woe and unrest.
> Thy friends are fled to wait upon thy foes
> And crossly to thy good all fortune goes.      *(lines 18–24)*

## Act 2 Critical review

The shift in Richard's fortunes has been dramatic. His seizure of Gaunt's land and possessions to finance his military campaign in Ireland and neutralise any future threat from Bullingbrook is a fatal miscalculation. Already deeply unhappy with Richard's increasingly autocratic style of government, the aristocracy are provoked beyond endurance by this blatantly unjust action.

Before he dies, Gaunt himself prophetically warns Richard of the folly of his behaviour, as does York. Northumberland, Ross and Willoughby privately voice similar criticisms. Scarcely has Richard departed for Ireland than news comes that Bullingbrook has returned to England at the head of an armed force which rapidly increases in strength as alienated nobles flock to join him. Even York, appointed Governor of England by Richard, begins to waver in his allegiance and the king's Welsh army melts away.

Act 2 presents a deeply unsympathetic portrait of Richard as a tyrant king, with his cold indifference to Gaunt's death and blatant disregard for Bullingbrook's legal right of inheritance. Yet even as Shakespeare makes clear the king's many follies and errors of policy he opens up a new perspective – the personal devotion that Richard could inspire in both friends and followers. His queen fears for his safety and the faithful Earl of Salisbury watches with 'eyes of heavy mind' as Richard's 'sun sets weeping in the lowly west'.

Bullingbrook's sun, however, is clearly rising and reports of his growing strength send waves of panic through Richard's supporters. Shakespeare shows him confidently greeting new supporters and skilfully countering York's legitimate concerns that he should be taking up arms against the crown. Even the elements seem to favour Bullingbrook as contrary winds prevent Richard's immediate return from Ireland to marshal his defence.

In this time of political crisis the language of the play rings with angry argument, accusation and listing of grievances. The muted and oblique criticism of the king in Act 1 has now become openly hostile. But, amidst this noisy political wrangling, new voices can be heard, uttering premonitions of change and disaster on an almost cosmic scale.

## Act 3 Scene 1

Bullingbrook's progress seems almost effortless. Bristol Castle has been captured. Bushy and Green are his prisoners. Before Bullingbrook pronounces sentence of death on them, he makes clear to all present that these executions are a matter of justice, not revenge. It is his first public display of king-like authority and his opening words are cold and blunt:

> Bushy and Green, I will not vex your souls,
> Since presently your souls must part your bodies    *(lines 2–3)*

First Bullingbrook accuses the king's advisers of misleading and corrupting 'a prince, a royal king', tempting him into 'sinful' practices that destroyed the royal marriage. Then, in words ringing with anger, he lists the injuries they have done to him. They turned the king against him and made him eat 'the bitter bread of banishment' (line 21). They took possession of his properties, his hunting parks and forests, obliterating completely his heraldic crests and coats of arms 'leaving me no sign / . . . / To show the world I am a gentleman' (lines 25–7).

Bushy and Green accept their fate with a defiant dignity and loyalty to Richard that is strangely at odds with earlier accusations of Northumberland and others that the king had been 'basely led / By flatterers' (Act 2 Scene 1, lines 241–2). Then, astutely demonstrating that he can also be compassionate, Bullingbrook asks his uncle to send kind greetings to the queen and ensure that she is properly treated. That York has already done as much (lines 40–1) merely confirms what the audience already suspects. York is now Bullingbrook's ally and counsellor, not his master.

Businesslike as ever, Bullingbrook prepares to engage with the king's Welsh allies, as yet unaware that they have already disbanded. Only then will Bullingbrook and his followers be able to relax: 'A while to work, and after holiday' (line 44). Many in Shakespeare's audience would have appreciated the irony of this remark, for the future King Henry IV's troubles are only just beginning (see pages 48 and 61).

## Act 3 Scene 2

A callous and erratic tyrant may have left for Ireland, but a rather different king returns, as Shakespeare begins to turn the audience's sympathies in Richard's favour. The king has at last managed to ship his army back from Ireland and landed at Barkloughly (Harlech) Castle on the west coast of Wales. He knows of Bullingbrook's rebellion but does not yet realise just how much of his support has ebbed away.

Unlike Bullingbrook's calculated, practical decisiveness, there is a strangely loving tenderness in Richard's expression of joy at returning to his beloved kingdom. Like a mother reunited with her child, he kneels to touch the ground, smiling and weeping (lines 4–11). The king speaks to the earth as if it were a living spirit, asking spiders, toads and nettles to impede the 'treacherous feet' of his rebellious enemies, and 'lurking adders' to 'throw death' upon them. Not even the obvious amusement of his companions at his strange behaviour can dent Richard's mystical sense of communion with his country:

> Mock not my senseless conjuration, lords.
> This earth shall have a feeling and these stones
> Prove armèd soldiers ere her native king
> Shall falter under foul rebellion's arms.          *(lines 23–6)*

But spiders, toads, nettles and adders will not stop an army. The Bishop of Carlisle respectfully, if somewhat convolutedly, reminds the king that he must take up every God-sent opportunity to save his crown (lines 27–32). Lord Aumerle, York's son, puts it more bluntly: the king is guilty of 'security' (overconfidence) and must act immediately to stem the ever-rising power of Bullingbrook, who grows ever 'strong and great in substance and in power' (line 35).

Richard, however, remains convinced his enemies will evaporate before the 'anointed' majesty of his royal person (lines 36–62). Bullingbrook and his followers are like thieves in the night (lines 51–3) who will stand 'bare and naked' when the sun of Richard returns to light the sky (the rising sun was the historical Richard's personal emblem). For, like Gaunt, Richard believes in a monarch's divine right to rule (see pages 70–1). No 'breath of worldly men' has power to depose the 'anointed king'. Richard is answerable only to God, who will, for every one of Bullingbrook's soldiers, provide the king with 'A glorious angel':

> Not all the water in the rough rude sea
> Can wash the balm off from an anointed king.

> The breath of worldly men cannot depose
> The deputy elected by the Lord.
> For every man that Bullingbrook hath pressed
> To lift shrewd steel against our golden crown
> God for His Richard hath in heavenly pay
> A glorious angel.                    *(lines 54–61)*

The poetic power and resonance of Richard's words would have stirred the hearts of many (although not all) in Shakespeare's audience, for it was a doctrine regularly preached in churches throughout the land on orders from the Tudor government (see pages 70–1). Unlike Elizabeth I, however, what Shakespeare's Richard has tragically failed to ensure is that his public image is backed up by military force.

Salisbury informs the king that he has returned just a day too late to prevent the dispersal of his entire Welsh army. The blood drains visibly from Richard's face (line 75), but at Aumerle's prompting the king manages to regain his composure by repeating the same divine right mantra as before in a kind of rhetorical show of bravado:

> I had forgot myself. Am I not king?
> Awake, thou coward! Majesty, thou sleepest.
> Is not the king's name twenty thousand names?    *(lines 83–5)*

Sir Stephen Scroope brings more unwelcome news. Bullingbrook, like a swollen river, has flooded England 'With hard bright steel and hearts harder than steel' (line 111). Old men, boys and even women have taken up arms against the king. Richard angrily demands to know why Bushy, Green, Bagot and the Earl of Wiltshire offered no resistance, suspecting that they have treacherously 'made peace' with Bullingbrook. Scroope's grimly ironic confirmation, 'Peace have they made with him indeed, my lord', sends Richard into another of his rages. He accuses his former advisers of being 'Three Judases', but their betrayal of him, he declares, is three times worse than Judas's betrayal of Christ (lines 129–34), until Scroope sardonically makes his meaning clear. Bushy, Green and the Earl of Wiltshire have made peace 'With heads and not with hands' (line 138).

As Richard takes in the significance of Scroope's news, his mood switches from soaring confidence to melodramatic despair. Unable to

face the intolerable reality of the loss of his kingdom, he takes refuge
in the comforting prospect of death:

> Let's talk of graves, of worms and epitaphs,
> Make dust our paper and with rainy eyes
> Write sorrow on the bosom of the earth.
> Let's choose executors and talk of wills.            *(lines 145–8)*

The king's imagination toys with images of the hollowness and
fragility of existence: how all man can really call his own is one small
grave covered with a thin crust of earth (lines 149–54), how history is
full of the 'sad stories of the death of kings':

> How some have been deposed, some slain in war,
> Some haunted by the ghosts they have deposed,
> Some poisoned by their wives, some sleeping killed,
> All murdered                                        *(lines 157–60)*

A king may believe himself invulnerable, Richard muses, but within
his 'hollow crown' sits Death, mocking his pomp and majesty,
allowing him one 'little scene / To monarchise', until 'with a little
pin' he pierces the king's 'castle wall' (lines 160–70). For the first
time in the play Richard accepts that he is vulnerable. Show me no
'solemn reverence', he says. I am just flesh and blood like any of my
subjects:

> I live with bread like you, feel want,
> Taste grief, need friends. Subjected thus,
> How can you say to me I am a king?                  *(lines 175–7)*

Events have clearly given Richard a wisdom that power and
prosperity could never teach him. The king's supporters, however,
need action not enlightenment. Carlisle and Aumerle attempt once
more to rally the king's spirits. The bishop urges Richard to fight
whatever the odds, for once the king gives way to fear he will certainly
be killed. His cousin urges him to seek the help of York, and Richard
responds, recovering something of his former bravado, until Scroope
reluctantly delivers his final piece of news. York has joined with
Bullingbrook, Richard's northern castles have surrendered and the

whole of southern England is in arms against the king (lines 194–203). Richard at once discharges the remains of his army and sinks into a mood of despairing self-pity. He will not even listen to Aumerle's final attempt to rouse his spirits. The title of sun-king now belongs to Bullingbrook:

> Discharge my followers, let them hence away
> From Richard's night to Bullingbrook's fair day.   *(lines 217–18)*

## Act 3 Scene 3

Shakespeare now switches the play's focus back to Bullingbrook. From Bristol, the duke has moved swiftly into Wales and is close by Flint Castle where, unknown to him, the king has taken refuge. Although the campaign is going to plan, there are tensions among the rebel leaders which come to the surface when Northumberland omits to use the king's title (line 6). This earns a sharp rebuke from York, who is clearly still unhappy with what the rebels are doing:

> It would beseem the Lord Northumberland
> To say King Richard. Alack the heavy day
> When such a sacred king should hide his head.   *(lines 7–9)*

When Northumberland assures him that he omitted Richard's title 'Only to be brief', York remarks that there was a time when the king would have 'shortened' Northumberland by a 'whole head's length' for showing such disrespect. Bullingbrook attempts to placate his uncle. Northumberland had just made a mistake, that was all. York then turns on his nephew, warning him to 'Take' only what is rightfully his, lest he 'mistake' (i.e. take unlawfully):

> Take not, good cousin, further than you should,
> Lest you mistake. The heavens are o'er our heads.   *(lines 16–17)*

Bullingbrook assures his uncle that he will not oppose heaven's 'will'. That God might 'will' the crown to come to *him* he is careful not to specify (lines 18–19).

Before Bullingbrook can speak further, Harry Percy arrives with news that Richard is lodged inside Flint Castle. The crucial confrontation between king and duke is imminent. Now more than ever, Bullingbrook must choose his words with care and the instructions he gives his emissary Northumberland are as much for the ears of his own supporters as for Richard (lines 31–50). First he pledges allegiance to Richard's 'most royal person', then promises to lay down his arms once the king has restored his former lands and titles. However, should the king refuse, Bullingbrook makes it brutally clear what he intends to do:

> If not I'll use the advantage of my power
> And lay the summer's dust with showers of blood
> Rained from the wounds of slaughtered Englishmen
>
> *(lines 42–4)*

As Northumberland leaves to negotiate with Richard, Bullingbrook assembles his forces in full view of Flint Castle. He clearly senses the significance of this moment. It is like the 'thundering shock' when the elemental forces of fire and water meet:

> Methinks King Richard and myself should meet
> With no less terror than the elements
> Of fire and water when their thundering shock
> At meeting tears the cloudy cheeks of heaven.
> Be he the fire, I'll be the yielding water.    *(lines 54–8)*

Trumpets sound from Northumberland's party calling for a 'parle' (truce) and are answered by trumpets from within the castle. A brief pause then a 'flourish' (fanfare) of trumpets to announce the entrance of the king. Many productions have highlighted the magnificence of Richard's appearance on the battlements, sometimes dressing him in dazzlingly rich and shimmering coronation robes.

Both Bullingbrook and York are moved by the king's air of command (lines 62–71). To Bullingbrook, Richard seems like 'the blushing discontented sun' (another elemental image); to York his eye is 'As bright as is the eagle's', sending forth 'Controlling' rays of majesty like bolts of lightning. It is as if Shakespeare is ironically showing the authority in Richard's appearance at the very moment his actual power is melting away.

The king waits, expecting Northumberland to kneel to him (lines 72–6). But in a silent gesture of rebellion, the earl refuses to do so. If

I am not your lawful sovereign, Richard tells him angrily, then show me proof that God's hand has 'dismissed us from our stewardship', for only He has power to 'gripe [seize] the sacred handle of our sceptre' (line 80):

> Yet know: my master, God omnipotent,
> Is mustering in his clouds on our behalf
> Armies of pestilence, and they shall strike
> Your children yet unborn and unbegot
> That lift your vassal hands against my head
> And threat the glory of my precious crown.  *(lines 85–90)*

Richard makes a prophecy: Bullingbrook's 'dangerous treason' will bequeath to England only 'bleeding war', and if he dares to seize the crown, the price will be 'Ten thousand bloody crowns of mothers' sons' to drench the grass of England 'with faithful English blood'. In response, Northumberland makes a show of apologetic regret, assuring the king that Bullingbrook has no rebellious intent, desiring only his 'lineal royalties' (hereditary rights). Once Bullingbrook has obtained 'Enfranchisement' (freedom from banishment) he will put away his arms and pledge 'faithful service' to his king (line 18).

Richard pretends to believe Northumberland's assurances. With smiling words he welcomes Bullingbrook's return to England and agrees to all of the duke's demands. Northumberland leaves silently and without ceremony. It galls Richard to be forced 'to speak so fair' to the likes of Northumberland and Bullingbrook. He wonders for a moment if he should not submit without a fight, but Aumerle counsels caution: 'Till time lend friends, and friends their helpful swords' (line 132).

The king, however, realises all too well that to rescind the sentence of banishment on 'yon proud man' Bullingbrook is to concede he is king only in name. His heart swells with grief (lines 133–41) as he waits nervously for Northumberland's return from Bullingbrook, already resigning himself to the fact that he will be deposed:

> What must the king do now? Must he submit?
> The king shall do it. Must he be deposed?
> The king shall be contented. Must he lose
> The name of king? A God's name let it go.  *(lines 143–6)*

Richard immediately seizes on the possibility of his deposition and contemplates almost longingly the new role in life he might now be required to play. Stage by stage, in a series of balanced antitheses, he charts the details of his imagined change from royal magnificence to humble man of God:

> I'll give my jewels for a set of beads,
> My gorgeous palace for a hermitage,
> My gay apparel for an almsman's gown,
> My figured goblets for a dish of wood,
> My sceptre for a palmer's walking staff,
> My subjects for a pair of carvèd saints,
> And my large kingdom for a little grave,
> A little, little grave, an obscure grave.          *(lines 147–54)*

Aumerle is moved to tears when he hears the king talk of being buried 'in the king's highway' where his 'subjects' feet / May hourly trample on their sovereign's head' as now they tread upon his heart. Moved by his cousin's distress, Richard attempts to comfort him. He jokingly imagines the two cousins carving with their joint tears a pair of graves with the epitaph 'There lies / Two kinsmen digged their graves with weeping eyes' (lines 168–9). The king's fanciful image even manages to provoke Aumerle to smile ruefully (lines 170–1).

The king now turns to Northumberland, addressing him sarcastically as 'Most mighty prince' and asking to know Bullingbrook's decision. Northumberland's apparently polite request that Richard should come down to the base (lower) court to meet Bullingbrook is full of menace. No king would obey a request from one of his subjects to come down to meet him. That subject would be required to come up to him.

Richard knows his descent to 'the base court' will signify public acceptance of his loss of power. In anguish and despair at the extent of his ruin, he repeatedly emphasises the words 'down' and 'base', imagining himself to be Phaëton, son of the god Apollo, struggling to control the horses ('jades') of his father's sun chariot as it plunges earthwards:

> Down, down I come, like glistering Phaëton,
> Wanting the manage of unruly jades.

> In the base court? Base court where kings grow base
> To come at traitors' calls and do them grace!
> In the base court come down. Down court, down king,
> For night owls shriek where mounting larks should sing.
>
> *(lines 178–83)*

Productions have highlighted this momentous 'fall' in many ways. In one late twentieth-century production, the central tower on which Richard stood spiralled to the ground. In another production, Richard's golden coronation cloak, which had hung suspended above the stage 'like a fourteen-sided sun', fluttered to the stage. Another Richard took off his white robe, slipped his crown over it and dropped both over the side of the castle wall, drawing everyone's eyes to their symbolic descent.

When Richard descends, Bullingbrook kneels to him and orders his followers to do the same. The king, however, rightly interprets this gesture as a mere show of 'courtesy' (in one production Northumberland remained standing). Get off your knees, he says to Bullingbrook, for your ambition reaches at least as high as to my crown:

> Me rather had my heart might feel your love
> Than my unpleased eye see your courtesy.
> Up, cousin, up. Your heart is up, I know,
> Thus high at least [*Pointing to his head*], although your knee be
>   low. *(lines 191–4)*

Although Bullingbrook continues to insist he comes only for what is rightfully his, Richard remains firmly convinced his cousin intends to depose him (lines 195–200). Finally the king takes the hands of his weeping uncle York and accepts the inevitable. Bullingbrook shall have his crown:

> What you will have I'll give, and willing too,
> For do we must what force will have us do. *(lines 205–6)*

It is unclear whether Bullingbrook had designs on Richard's crown before this meeting, but the duke must surely be considering it now.

# Act 3 Scene 4

This scene in the Duke of York's garden is a strangely unique moment in the play, placed as it is between the momentous shift in power at Flint Castle and Richard's public abdication in Act 4. Here, seemingly far away from the great affairs of state, Shakespeare prompts the audience to reflect on how a king should govern well, something which Richard has clearly failed to do.

Starved of news about her husband, the queen looks for some 'sport' (entertainment) to 'drive away the heavy thought of care' (line 2), but nothing her attendant ladies can suggest will serve. One gentlewoman even offers to weep for her mistress if that would console her. If weeping could make me happy, the queen replies, my own tears would already have cured my grief (lines 21–3)

When three gardeners arrive to work in the garden, the queen decides to listen in on their conversation, certain that they will discuss the latest political situation ('talk of state'):

> My wretchedness unto a row of pins
> They'll talk of state, for everyone doth so
> Against a change. Woe is forerun with woe.        *(lines 26–8)*

Gaunt had famously described England as a garden ('This other Eden'). Now the Gardener speaks as if his garden were a country and he the tutor of future princes on how to govern well (lines 29–39). He instructs his assistants to support and nurture the 'young dangling apricocks', but 'like an executioner' cut off the heads of plants that grow too fast, for 'All must be even in our government.' He himself, meanwhile, must 'root away / The noisome [harmful] weeds' that drain the goodness from the ground. One of his assistants makes the inevitable link with the present sorry state of England (lines 40–7). Why should we keep our garden well-ordered, he says,

> When our sea-wallèd garden, the whole land,
> Is full of weeds, her fairest flowers choked up,
> Her fruit trees all unpruned, her hedges ruined,
> Her knots [flowerbeds] disordered and her wholesome herbs
> Swarming with caterpillars?        *(lines 43–7)*

In words that clearly echo Bullingbrook's threat (Act 2 Scene 3, lines

165–6) to 'weed and pluck away' the 'caterpillars of the commonwealth', the Gardener describes how the duke 'plucked up root and all' the king's advisers, those 'weeds . . . / That seemed in eating him to hold him up' and took 'the wasteful king' prisoner. If only Richard had, like a good gardener, ringed and pruned the country's fruit trees, he could have controlled and cut back the 'great and growing men' who threatened the security of his kingdom.

The queen can stay silent no longer. She angrily confronts the Gardener, demanding to know how he came by 'this ill tidings'. Reluctantly he explains, using an image that encapsulates the essential pattern of the whole play. Richard is in Bullingbrook's power, both men are now weighed in Fortune's scales and Richard has been found wanting (lines 84–9).

The distraught queen prepares to go to London to meet Richard, cursing the Gardener for bringing her such evil news. The Gardener may disapprove of the king's bad government, but he cannot help but feel 'ruth' (pity) for the 'weeping queen'. He resolves to plant a bed of herbs to commemorate this sad occasion:

> Here did she fall a tear. Here in this place
> I'll set a bank of rue, sour herb of grace.
> Rue even for ruth here shortly shall be seen
> In the remembrance of a weeping queen.          *(lines 104–7)*

## Act 3 Critical review

As the epic confrontation between king and duke draws ever closer and the king's forces inexorably decline, Shakespeare shows how a monarch, accustomed from childhood to command, struggles to deal with defeat and loss of power.

Richard is at first strangely passive in his response to the threat from Bullingbrook, irrationally confident that God will protect his anointed royal personage. Successive reports of the grim reality of his situation only provoke him to outbursts of paralysed despair. But if Richard's remaining friends and supporters are exasperated by his passivity and defeatism, they are also deeply moved by the king's powerful evocations of the fragile transience of worldly success and happiness. It is as though Richard finds a kind of comfort in imagining himself set free from the heavy cares of state.

The confrontation between Richard and Bullingbrook at Flint Castle is the play's pivotal point. Political control of England changes hands and Richard's royal authority finally ebbs away. Bullingbrook anticipates this moment as like the 'thundering shock' of lightning as it 'tears the cloudy cheeks of heaven'. As Richard descends to the base court 'like glistering Phaëton', he too senses a seismic shift of power and concedes the crown before Bullingbrook even ventures to demand it.

The allegorical garden scene provides a momentary pause in the onward sweep of events, inviting the audience to reflect on the essential qualities required for good government. If Richard's queen views her husband's kingdom as some kind of earthly paradise created by God for the royal couple's personal pleasure, the gardener is brutally practical. A successful prince must be wise, firm and diligent if he is to maintain an ordered and harmonious country – King Richard was foolish, idle and wasteful.

In this pivotal act, elemental images of earth, air, fire and water (sun, fire, lightning, floods, rivers, thunderstorms, tears, gardens, dust, graves) become increasingly insistent. They combine with images of blood and death to create a sense of ominously momentous change.

# Act 4 Scene 1

Bullingbrook has called a special parliamentary session of the nobility to investigate the circumstances of Gloucester's death. As the stage direction implies ('*Enter as to the Parliament*'), this is not a legitimate assembly, for only the king could legally preside over such proceedings. Historical records say that the king's empty Chair of State in Westminster Hall was covered over with a cloth of gold, a visible reminder of the unresolved monarchical crisis.

This scene is in many ways a mirror image of the play's opening where King Richard heard the charges and counter-charges between Bullingbrook and Mowbray. Now it is Bullingbrook who must act to keep the peace between 'High stomached' nobles. Bagot, one of Richard's former advisers, is summoned to reveal what he knows of Gloucester's death, who persuaded the king to sanction it and who carried out the killing.

Bagot, presumably turned informer to save his own neck, accuses Aumerle not only of carrying out Gloucester's murder but also wishing for Bullingbrook's death or permanent exile (lines 8–19). In characteristically aristocratic fashion, Aumerle calls Bagot a liar and throws down his gage to challenge him to Trial by Combat, even though it will dishonour his 'fair stars' (high birth) to fight on equal terms with such a 'base' (lower ranked) man as Bagot (lines 19–29).

When Bullingbrook moves swiftly to prevent Bagot from taking up the challenge, Aumerle turns on the assembled nobility to challenge any of them to fight him. Lord Fitzwater hurls down his gage, as does Northumberland's son, Harry Percy, and another lord (lines 33–56). Aumerle's response is to challenge every single noble in the hall to battle (lines 57–9). He is not without supporters. The Duke of Surrey calls Fitzwater a liar and also challenges him to combat. In response, Fitzwater claims the banished Mowbray said that Aumerle had sent two men to Calais to kill Gloucester. By now Aumerle has no more gages left to hurl and has to borrow one to challenge the absent Mowbray should he ever be 'repealed' (called back from exile) (lines 83–5).

Some productions have cut this sequence of the brawling lords, fearing it might seem too farcical. Even an Elizabethan audience must have found the flurry of gages being thrown down amusingly archaic. The truth is, historical records confirm that such an episode did occur and that Aumerle received 21 challenges in all. In a dispute between nobles earlier in Richard's reign, 305 gages were thrown at the feet of one unfortunate lord. An observer wrote that the descending gloves 'looked like a fall of snow'.

To prevent the situation escalating out of control, Bullingbrook declares that all disputes between the Lords Appellant must wait until Mowbray is recalled from banishment (lines 86–90). Whereupon the Bishop of Carlisle announces that the Duke of Norfolk has died after honourably fighting as a crusader for 'his captain, Christ', in campaigns against 'black pagans, Turks and Saracens' (see page 67).

Everything that has happened so far is merely prologue to the main event: the legal transfer of power from Richard to Bullingbrook. Parliament must be convinced that Richard voluntarily relinquishes his crown, for there was no legal method by which medieval subjects could depose their king. Right on cue, York enters to announce that Richard has voluntarily abdicated the throne in favour of Bullingbrook (lines 107–12).

One member, at least, of the assembly is unconvinced. Before Bullingbrook can 'In God's name . . . ascend the regal throne' (line 113), the Bishop of Carlisle vehemently protests the illegality of deposing their divinely appointed monarch: 'Marry, God forbid!' (line 114). He may be the 'Worst' (lowest ranked) of the nobility assembled there, the bishop says, but not even the most 'noble' of those present is 'enough noble' to pass judgement on 'noble Richard' (lines 117–22). Even the most obviously guilty thief has the right to be present at his trial, the bishop argues, so God 'forfend' (forbid) that 'subject and inferior breath' should judge the king when he is not even present (lines 123–31). Bullingbrook, 'whom you call king', is a mere subject and therefore 'foul traitor' to the rightful king:

> And if you crown him let me prophesy:
> The blood of English shall manure the ground
> And future ages groan for this foul act.        *(lines 136–8)*

The bishop's prophetic vision of an England at war with itself ('kin with kin and kind with kind') would have been all too real to an Elizabethan audience who above all feared the return of civil war (see pages 70–1). How many of the nobles present are likewise moved by Carlisle's warning? There are at least two, as the audience will later learn (lines 320–33). But Northumberland moves decisively to silence further public dissent. He arrests the bishop on charges of 'capital treason' and asks the assembled lords to 'grant the commons' suit' (a request from the House of Commons to learn the details of Richard's abdication). Bullingbrook, however, interrupts him, alerted perhaps by the bishop's outburst to the need for Richard to be seen to abdicate. He therefore orders the king to be brought before the assembly:

> Fetch hither Richard, that in common view
> He may surrender. So we shall proceed
> Without suspicion. *(lines 155–7)*

When the king enters, he speaks like a beaten man, asking Bullingbrook for time to learn 'submission', 'To insinuate, flatter, bow and bend [his] knee' as a subject should. Yet when Richard turns to face the assembled nobility there is power in his words. They all once had hailed him king, but now, like Judas, they have betrayed their Christ:

> Yet I well remember
> The favours of these men. Were they not mine?
> Did they not sometime cry 'All hail' to me?
> So Judas did to Christ, but he in twelve
> Found truth in all but one, I in twelve thousand none.
> *(lines 167–71)*

The reproach strikes home, for Richard's royal salute to Bullingbrook is followed by an uncomfortable, guilty silence (lines 172–5). Perhaps the nobles' discomfort gives Richard hope. Words had little power against Bullingbrook's army, but might yet move the hearts and minds of Parliament. If Richard must abdicate, he will do so on his own terms. He calls for his crown and holds it out for Bullingbrook to take, but tightens his grip on the symbol of power at the very moment the duke takes hold of it. Bullingbrook, who dare not be seen to 'seize the crown', is therefore caught helpless in this moment of fine balance, while Richard constructs an elaborate verbal image of their interlocked fortunes like two buckets in a well:

> Give me the crown. Here, cousin, seize the crown,
> On this side my hand and on that side thine.

> Now is this golden crown like a deep well
> That owes two buckets, filling one another,
> The emptier ever dancing in the air,
> The other down, unseen and full of water.
> That bucket, down and full of tears, am I,
> Drinking my griefs whilst you mount up on high.
>
> *(lines 181–8)*

Bullingbrook, anxious for the ceremony to appear not only legal but smooth and uncomplicated, tries several times to cajole the king into resigning the crown. But Richard is too full of the realisation of what he is about to lose to give an unequivocal answer. For without his title Richard will have nothing except his grief. He will lose his very identity. He will *be* nothing (lines 189–201). Even when at last he manages to answer yes, his hesitant punning reply (playing on 'aye' and 'I') suggests that he still wishes his 'yes' could be a 'no':

> Aye – no. No – aye, for I must nothing be,
> Therefore no 'no', for I resign to thee.     *(lines 200–1)*

To further heighten the sense of ritual created by the rhymes in this exchange between Richard and Bullingbrook (lines 187–201) and to make absolutely clear the enormity of what is being required of him, Richard now proceeds to conduct a kind of inverted coronation ceremony where he 'unkings' himself, first surrendering his crown and sceptre, then symbolically washing away the 'balm' (oil) with which he had been anointed, releasing his subjects from their oaths of allegiance, giving up his properties and cancelling all laws passed in his name. As Richard makes his abdication statement, its formalistic style, with repeated phrase patterns and balanced end-stopped lines (see pages 86–7), creates a sense of momentous change:

> Now, mark me how I will undo myself.
> I give this heavy weight from off my head
> And this unwieldy sceptre from my hand,
> The pride of kingly sway from out my heart.
> With mine own tears I wash away my balm;
> With mine own hands I give away my crown;
> With mine own tongue deny my sacred state;

With mine own breath release all duteous oaths.
All pomp and majesty I do forswear;
My manors, rents, revenues I forgo;
My acts, decrees, and statutes I deny.
God pardon all oaths that are broke to me;
God keep all vows unbroke are made to thee.     *(lines 202–14)*

Richard concludes his statement of abdication by wishing for his 'unkinged' self an early death and for the new king a long reign with 'many years of sunshine days'. In a French production of the play (directed by Mnouchkine, 1981), Richard was dressed in a multi-layered series of red, white and gold vestments, rather like a high priest. As he made his abdication speech, black-robed attendants helped him take off the outward signs of his royal status, so that, as each layer was stripped away, Richard became progressively smaller and more vulnerable, while Bullingbrook gained in physical stature as he took on the royal robes of authority.

Bullingbrook, however, still has to prove to the assembly that Richard is unfit to govern. When, therefore, the king asks 'What more remains?', Northumberland demands that he publicly confess to a list of 'accusations' and 'grievous crimes' to prove that he has been 'worthily deposed' (lines 221–6). This final humiliation is too much for Richard. 'And must I ravel out / My weaved-up follies?', he asks Northumberland, challenging him to consider that he would be ashamed to read a list of his own 'offences'; indeed, 'one heinous Article' Northumberland could be accused of would concern 'the deposing of a king' (line 233). Richard turns once again to confront the assembled lords with a biblical parallel. Like Judas, they have betrayed their Christ (line 170) and now, like Pilate, they are washing their hands of any responsibility for their king's fate, his 'sour cross' (lines 236–41).

None of this moves Northumberland. He repeats his request to 'Read o'er' the Articles without delay. But the king's eyes are too full of tears to see anything but his own treachery to himself and his 'Proud majesty', which makes him no different to the 'sort [gang] of traitors' assembled before him. No longer can he call himself Northumberland's lord, 'Nor no man's lord', for he has neither name nor title, only a yearning for oblivion, to be able to melt away like a snowman in the winter sun:

> Oh that I were a mockery king of snow
> Standing before the sun of Bullingbrook,
> To melt myself away in water drops. *(lines 259–61)*

Then, suddenly and disconcertingly, Richard asks for a looking glass to be brought 'That it may show me what a face I have'. Bullingbrook grants his wish at once, perhaps hoping to humour him, perhaps genuinely pitying the deposed king's distress. While they wait for the servant to return with the mirror, the relentless Northumberland yet again urges Richard to confess to the 'Articles', but the prospect of further public humiliation so enrages Richard that Bullingbrook orders the earl to desist (lines 268–70). Richard assures them both (presumably when the looking glass he has called for arrives) that he will be happy to read the sins that 'are writ' upon his very being, or soul:

> They [the commons] shall be satisfied. I'll read enough
> When I do see the very book indeed
> Where all my sins are writ, and that's my self. *(lines 272–4)*

Many critics and actors regard the 'looking-glass' episode which follows as the pivotal point in Richard's transformation from proud consecrated king to humble victim tragically aware of his own mortality. It is not easy, however, to catch and fix this episode's puzzling, shifting meanings, for the looking glass signified at least two very different sets of qualities. Since it reflected physical appearance and flattered the gazer, it symbolised self-obsessed vanity, superficiality and pride. Elizabethans, however, also believed a mirror had the ability to reflect the divine light from a person's soul, thus symbolising self-awareness, wisdom and truth.

Richard's mirror seems both to flatter and speak truth. When he first looks merely at his outward appearance, he is almost disappointed that the face he sees shows no trace of sorrow's 'wounds'. Clearly this is a 'flattering glass', deceiving him just as his followers did in his prosperity:

> Give me that glass and therein will I read.
> No deeper wrinkles yet? Hath sorrow struck
> So many blows upon this face of mine

And made no deeper wounds? Oh flattering glass,
Like to my followers in prosperity
Thou dost beguile me.                                    *(lines 275–80)*

This realisation prompts him to look at his reflection as if it were an image from a different world and time, sent to remind him of all the 'follies' he once 'faced' (covered up, condoned) when he was king, until he was 'outfaced' (overcome) by Bullingbrook. Then, in a dramatic gesture of anger and despair, he breaks the glass, as if to demonstrate both to himself and to the new king just how fragile and vulnerable earthly power can be (lines 286–90).

So far in this scene, as Richard observes, Bullingbrook has indeed been a 'silent king', apparently unmoved by Richard's emotional tricks, keeping his distance, letting Northumberland do the political 'dirty work' for him. Now, at last, he is drawn into responding to his cousin's riddling word games, so that when Richard compares the shattering of his reflection in the mirror to sorrow's destruction of his real identity, Bullingbrook replies equally enigmatically:

The shadow of your sorrow hath destroyed
The shadow of your face.                                 *(lines 291–2)*

It is not clear whether Bullingbrook intends to comfort Richard (i.e. the mirror has only broken his image, not his true self) or to sneer at him (i.e. his sorrow may be genuine but its expression is theatrical – a playing with shadows). Deborah Warner's 1995 National Theatre production with Fiona Shaw as Richard (see page 102) had Bullingbrook respond to Richard's breaking of the mirror with a genuine, almost brotherly compassion. John Barton's 1973 production, in contrast (see page 101), turned this moment into an emblem of Richard's life and death. After the deposed king had punched out the glass in frustration, Bullingbrook lifted the circular frame, slowly placing it over Richard's head so that it became first a halo, then a crown and finally a noose.

Whatever Bullingbrook intends to say, Richard seizes on his words to invest the shadow image with his own personal meaning. Richard's outer forms of grief ('these external manners of laments') may indeed be mere shows or 'shadows' to his 'unseen grief', but that inner grief is very real (lines 292–7). With bitter irony, Richard thanks the new king for his 'great bounty' in teaching him such a valuable lesson, then requests one final 'boon' (favour). When Bullingbrook assures him he has only to 'Name it, fair cousin', Richard is again fulsomely and sarcastically grateful (lines 304–8).

Suddenly Richard seems to tire of playing this game of words. He asks leave to go, no matter where so long as it is from the sight of Bullingbrook and his supporters. Ever the politician, Bullingbrook orders his men to 'convey' (escort) Richard to the security of the Tower of London. His use of the word 'convey' sparks one final bitter comment from Richard on what the assembled lords have done to him, for 'convey' could also mean 'transfer the legal ownership of property', or 'thieve, steal' (lines 315–17). This will be the last time the two great rivals speak to each other. Ignoring Richard's final outburst, Bullingbrook announces to the assembly the date of his coronation and Richard is led off under guard.

As the assembly of nobles disperse, three men remain behind. Lord Aumerle and the Bishops of Westminster and Carlisle are not just deeply unhappy with the new regime, they are more than ready to do something about it (lines 320–4). It was not unusual in the late fourteenth century for 'holy clergymen' to be actively involved in affairs of state. The House of Lords included many powerful prelates like Carlisle and Westminster. The latter almost seems to relish the prospect of plotting against the new King Henry:

> I see your brows are full of discontent,
> Your hearts of sorrow and your eyes of tears.
> Come home with me to supper. I will lay
> A plot shall show us all a merry day.          *(lines 330–3)*

If the audience has pitied Richard in this scene, they may feel some pity too for Henry Bullingbrook, as opposition to him grows even before he has been crowned. Indeed, as Shakespeare demonstrates in the sequel plays, *King Henry IV Parts 1 and 2*, this usurping king will discover all too well how 'Uneasy lies the head that wears a crown' (*King Henry IV Part 2* Act 3 Scene 1, line 31).

King of England in all but name, Bullingbrook presides over a special parliamentary assembly of the nobles, which quickly degenerates into a brawl of challenge and counter-challenge, providing a dramatic reminder of the unruly nature of the aristocratic class which Richard struggled to control and with which Bullingbrook must now grapple.

All this is prelude to the main event – the announcement of Richard's voluntary abdication and the proclaiming of Bullingbrook as his rightful heir. But what Bullingbrook had hoped to be mere formality is prevented by the Bishop of Carlisle's brave and solitary protest. The duke is therefore forced to summon Richard in person to the assembly to confirm the legitimacy of his abdication.

As he confronts the massed ranks of English lords, Richard at last discovers an inner strength, which enables him to turn the occasion into a moving ceremony of usurpation, a public demonstration that the rightful king is being deposed. Using all his verbal brilliance and theatrical skills, Richard holds his audience captive, forcing them to comprehend the enormity of what is taking place. Yet this is also an intensely personal performance, an attempt to understand himself and the nature of his 'hidden grief', to retain a hold on his sanity and sense of identity, to remember the man of power he once was.

Having witnessed the Bishop of Carlisle's arrest for 'capital treason', the remaining lords are significantly silent in the face of Richard's challenge. Even Bullingbrook seems ill at ease and increasingly the 'silent king'. Only the relentless Northumberland persists in his demands that Richard publicly confess his crimes. Shakespeare's focus now is very much on Richard's personal distress and the tragedy of his deposition. Bullingbrook may gain the crown but Richard captures the audience's sympathy.

The deposition sequence is memorable for its powerful fusion of poetry and drama: the image of twin buckets in a well as the former and future kings hold the crown between them; the heavily patterned ceremonial verse with which Richard accompanies the removal of his symbols of office; and the mirror that prompts his meditation on how flattering appearance so easily belies the reality of 'unseen grief'.

# Act 5 Scene 1

Richard's queen waits with her attendant ladies in one of the streets leading to the Tower, hoping to catch a glimpse of her husband as he is led into captivity. When the deposed king appears under guard, the queen cannot bear to see how much her 'fair rose' has withered (one production had Richard held by a long chain around his neck). She orders her companions to turn their eyes away from the sorry sight yet immediately urges them to look again so that together their 'true love tears' might 'wash him fresh again'. To the queen, Richard is like the 'model' (ruins) of a great city, like the stone effigy on a tomb, like a beautiful inn where 'hard-favoured grief' has come to stay, while victory resides with Bullingbrook at some cheap alehouse (lines 11–15).

In performance, the queen usually moves to take her husband's hand, but Richard stops her, for such a mingling of pleasure and pain would be unbearable. Instead he tells her that she must think of their former life as a 'happy dream' from which they have both been awakened to face the real world of 'grim Necessity'. Richard therefore urges the queen to seek refuge in France in 'some religious house'. Only new lives of Christian holiness can hope to win them heavenly crowns to replace the earthly crowns they have lost through their 'profane hours' (foolish and wicked behaviour) (lines 22–5). In response, the queen attempts to rouse her husband out of his despairing apathy. The lion, king of beasts, will roar defiance even when mortally wounded. So too should he (lines 26–34).

Richard, however, cannot be persuaded. There seems no more fight left in him. Again he tells his queen she must prepare to leave for France and reconcile herself to the fact that she will never see him alive again. He asks of her just one last promise. When in time to come she sits by the winter fire listening to 'good old folks' tell sad stories of long ago, before she bids them goodnight she must match their stories with 'the lamentable tale' of Richard and 'send the hearers weeping to their beds' (lines 40–5).

The king's self-indulgent, yet strangely moving, musings on the pathos of his situation are interrupted by the arrival of Northumberland. Bullingbrook, he informs him, has changed his mind (significantly omitting his new king's title just as he failed to kneel in respect to Richard at Flint Castle). Richard is to be taken to 'Pomfret' (Pontefract) Castle in Yorkshire and the queen must leave immediately for France. If the queen's criticisms had failed to rouse

Richard's spirits, the mere presence of Northumberland is provocation enough. He accuses the earl of being the 'ladder' by which Bullingbrook ascended his throne, and perceptively prophesies how their new alliance will quickly fall apart (lines 59–65).

Northumberland's response is brutally indifferent: 'My guilt be on my head, and there an end' (line 69). He orders Richard and his queen to say their farewells and part immediately. Richard feels himself 'Doubly divorced', first from his kingdom and now from his wife. Again he attempts to turn the moment into a kind of 'abdication' ceremony, but as he 'unkisses' his marriage vows he realises that the ties of love, like those of kingship, cannot easily be undone:

> Let me unkiss the oath twixt thee and me –
> And yet not so, for with a kiss 'twas made.          *(lines 74–5)*

The balanced, antithetical rhyming couplets with which Richard and his queen make their final farewells (lines 81–102) create a lyrical sense of shared suffering and parted love, while in the background the cynically political Northumberland waits. The queen begs the earl to allow Richard to join her in France, but Northumberland knows full well it would be 'little policy' (politically unwise) to allow Richard to remain at large, a constant threat to the new regime's security. Nor can Richard allow the queen's request to go with him. To have her nearby yet be forbidden to see her ('Better far off than, near, be ne'er the near') would be doubly unbearable.

They take one final kiss, then another, before they part to go their separate ways. Their obviously deep and mutual love must make an audience once again question the truth of Bullingbrook's allegation (Act 3 Scene 1, lines 11–15) that Richard's advisers had 'Broke the possession of a royal bed'. The queen takes no further part in the play. Like the Duchess of Gloucester (Act 1 Scene 2) she has been a powerless spectator of events. Many modern critics, however, see these women (together with the Duchess of York, who appears in the next scene) as offering an important feminine perspective on the very masculine world of politics and public life (see pages 74–5).

# Act 5 Scene 2
The Duke of York has been telling his wife how Richard and Bullingbrook were greeted by the people when they returned to

London from Flint Castle. But he became so upset when he remembered how the citizens of London 'Threw dust and rubbish on King Richard's head' that he could not go on (lines 1–6). Now that he has recovered somewhat, the duchess asks him to continue. Through York's story, Shakespeare paints a powerfully moving picture of the two cousins' entry into the capital.

First the duke describes Bullingbrook's triumphal entrance (lines 7–21), riding a 'hot and fiery steed' which seemed to sense the importance of its rider and hold itself in check. People thronged the windows to catch a glimpse of him and call out their support. As the bareheaded duke rode past he bowed low and thanked them humbly.

The duchess's sympathies, however, are with Richard and she asks her husband where the former king was all this while. The duke, deeply moved by the crowd's hostility to Richard and the patient dignity with which he bore his humiliation, uses the theatrical image of actors entering and leaving the stage to describe the hostile reception the defeated king received:

> As in a theatre the eyes of men
> After a well-graced actor leaves the stage
> Are idly bent on him that enters next,
> Thinking his prattle to be tedious,
> Even so or with much more contempt men's eyes
> Did scowl on Richard.                    (lines 23–8)

York, who had with such difficulty withdrawn his support from Richard, clearly still retains something of his former loyalty and struggles to reconcile himself to the new order of things (lines 37–40). They are all 'sworn subjects now' to Bullingbrook, he says, and must submit themselves to the will of heaven.

Their talk is interrupted by the arrival from Oxford of their son, once Duke of Aumerle but now deprived of his dukedom for supporting Richard. Aumerle might even have been executed had not York guaranteed his son's 'truth / And lasting fealty' (loyalty) to the new king (lines 44–5), a fact which York advises him to remember well (lines 50–1). As they talk, the duke notices that Aumerle has a document with a seal hidden inside his shirt. Suspicious as to why his son is so unwilling to divulge its contents, he pulls the paper from its hiding place and reads it. What it contains sends York into a furious rage. Accusing his son of treason and treachery, he calls for his horse to be saddled and his riding boots to be brought.

The bewildered duchess asks to know what the matter is but all the duke will say is that he intends to go to the new king to 'appeach [inform against] the villain' (line 79). When her son tells her that the contents of the document are enough to have him killed, she leaps at once to her son's defence before she even knows the details of his crime, ordering away the servant bringing the riding boots and pleading with her husband not to do anything to harm Aumerle (lines 85–93).

Even when York tells her that the document is proof her son was part of a 'dark conspiracy' to assassinate King Henry at Oxford, the duchess still begs York to be merciful to his son (lines 101–9). But York will not stay to listen. He hastens away to inform King Henry of the plot against his life. The duchess urges Aumerle to take his father's horse and get to the king first to ask for pardon. She will follow behind as fast as she is able.

# Act 5 Scene 3

King Henry is in conference with his advisers and as yet unaware of the Oxford conspiracy. He is concerned about his son, Prince Hal, who is not behaving as an heir to the throne should. He has been absent from court for three months, spending his time instead in taverns with thieves and other 'unrestrainèd loose companions' (line 7). The king's concern for the behaviour of his 'unthrifty' (extravagant), 'wanton' (unrestrained) and 'effeminate' son clearly echoes the earlier criticisms of the 'rash' and 'unstaid' (wild, uncontrolled) Richard (Act 2 Scene 1). Critics regard this mention of Prince Hal (who does not appear in the play) as a strong indication that Shakespeare already had sequel plays in mind, dealing with how both King Henry IV and the future King Henry V cope with the responsibilities of kingship (see pages 62–3).

The meeting is disturbed by the entrance of Aumerle, '*amazed*' (distraught), begging to be allowed a private conference with the king. Once alone, Aumerle falls to his knees and begs to be pardoned, which Henry agrees to do, provided Aumerle's crime was merely intended and not yet committed. Knowing his father to be close behind him, Aumerle asks permission to lock the door so he can tell his story undisturbed, but as soon as he does York is heard hammering to be let in and warning the king that there is a traitor with him. The king draws his sword, fearing an attempt on his life, but Aumerle assures him he is in no danger.

As soon as York gains access to the king, he shows him the document with the signatures of the conspirators. Aumerle begs him to remember his promise to pardon him and assures him that when he signed he never intended to go through with the assassination attempt. But York is implacable in his desire to have Aumerle brought to justice. His son fully intended to kill the king and only repented out of fear.

What follows is a series of contrasting perspectives on the conflicting loyalties created by Richard's deposition. Aumerle, faithful to the old king, is branded a traitor by the new; while York, deserter of the old king, is hailed as 'loyal father'. Yet when Henry declares that York's 'overflow of good' is enough to cleanse the 'defiled' waters of his son and earn him a royal pardon, the father feels he has been shamed. Only by his 'treacherous' son's death can the 'loyal' York live with honour: 'Mine honour lives when his dishonour dies' (line 69).

York's anguished expression of personal shame is cut short by the sound of his wife's voice outside the door. Despite the seriousness of Aumerle's crime, Henry seems to find it rather amusing to have yet another member of York's family pleading to be allowed to speak to him, likening it to something out of 'The Beggar and the King' (a popular Elizabethan ballad). The entry of the duchess, however, presents the audience with a new and maternal perspective on this male world of honour and dishonour. Immediately she falls to her knees and pleads desperately for her son's life, refusing to obey the king's command for her to rise.

In a play full of symbolically significant kneelings, Shakespeare now presents the picture of an entire family on their knees before the king. First Aumerle falls to his knees to beg for his life, followed by York to beg for his son's death. As elsewhere in this scene, the rhyming couplets create an undignified, almost farcical mood. The duchess, however, fears no loss of dignity as she desperately attempts to save her son (lines 99–109). York means not what he says. He 'prays but faintly', while she and her son 'pray with heart and soul and all beside'.

Not even her husband's mocking interruption can halt her. His sarcastic suggestion that the king should say 'pardonne moy', the

French for 'excuse me, forgive me' (for refusing her request), is met with a dignified rebuke. Why, the duchess asks, does York use the word 'pardon' to destroy his son's last hope of pardon? Seeing her husband begin to relent, she begs him to listen to his heart and join them in begging for the life of their son not the honour of his father.

The king, who has long ago decided to pardon Aumerle (lines 60–5), yet again asks his aunt to rise, but she will still not do so until she actually hears the king speak the word 'pardon'. Even when Henry does as much, she asks him to repeat it to be sure and seems comically and pathetically grateful in her response, addressing him as 'A god on earth' (line 135).

The king is not so merciful with the rest of the conspirators, however. His 'trusty brother-in-law' the Duke of Exeter, the Abbot of Westminster, together with 'all the rest of that consorted crew' are to be hunted down:

> They shall not live within this world, I swear,
> But I will have them if I once know where.       *(lines 141–2)*

## Act 5 Scene 4

This, the shortest scene in the play, with its succinct portrayal of how murderous ambition is spawned in the murky world of realpolitik, has been called 'a miniature dramatic masterpiece'. The discovery of the conspiracy to kill the king at Oxford has effectively sealed Richard's fate. Even shut away in Pomfret Castle, he is too much of a threat to King Henry to be allowed to live.

Sir Piers of Exton, looking to gain advancement with the new regime, has interpreted Henry's oblique comments about Richard as a clear instruction to have him killed:

> Didst thou not mark the king, what words he spake?
> 'Have I no friend will rid me of this living fear?'
>
> *(lines 1–2)*

Again the audience may sense an echo of the opening of the play. Might this be how Richard intimated to Mowbray that he desired the death of Gloucester? Richard never admitted to ordering the killing of his uncle. Will Henry be equally evasive about the killing of his cousin?

# Act 5 Scene 5

Richard, once the king 'not born to sue, but to command', waits helpless and alone in a prison cell in Pomfret Castle. Until now, there has always been an audience to listen to his words, to watch him play, by turns, the roles of just king, all-powerful king, betrayed king or fallen king. Here, on an empty stage, he speaks for the first time in soliloquy as he attempts to construct a new identity from the ruins of his former greatness.

He has already attempted to explore the parallels between the world he has lost and the prison he is in (lines 1–5), but has been unable to do it, for the world is full of people, while here there is only himself. Nevertheless, he will keep trying to 'hammer't out'. In an elaborate comparison (or 'conceit' see page 78), he imagines his brain and soul together breeding ever multiplying generations of thought-people to fill his solitary world, each thought possessing its own 'humour' or temperament.

But Richard's thoughts, like real people, can never find contentment. His 'better sort' of thoughts, like thoughts of heaven, are always mixed with 'scruples' (doubts) that see puzzling contradictions in God's words (lines 11–17). Ambitious thoughts plan 'Unlikely wonders', like escaping from this prison and, because they cannot, 'die in their own pride' (lines 18–22). Thoughts 'tending to content' (acceptance, resignation) seek comfort in the knowledge that they are not alone in suffering at the hands of Fortune (lines 23–30).

Yet these imaginatively fanciful musings, which have been so typical of Richard since his return from Ireland, paradoxically lead him to the painful realisation that he has been all these things: proud, doubting, unrealistically ambitious, too easily prone to despair, consistent only in his inconsistency. Now he both feels and understands that he is just a man like other men, swayed by conflicting and contradictory desires, happy with 'nothing' until death, the final 'nothing', shall come to ease his pain:

> Thus play I in one person many people,
> And none contented. Sometimes am I king,
> Then treasons make me wish myself a beggar,
> And so I am. Then crushing penury
> Persuades me I was better when a king,
> Then am I kinged again, and by and by

Think that I am unkinged by Bullingbrook,
And straight am nothing. But whate'er I be
Nor I nor any man that but man is
With nothing shall be pleased till he be eased
With being nothing.                    *(lines 31–41)*

Shakespeare underscores this significant moment by the playing of music. For a moment the unseen musicians' harmonies seem to echo Richard's new-found wisdom, but all too soon the music falters and the tune is broken. How strange, Richard muses (lines 41–8), that I can detect the discord in 'a disordered string' yet failed to hear the breaking of my own life's 'concord' (harmony).

This notion of musical time leads Richard to weave a second elaborate image: 'I wasted time and now doth time waste me' (lines 49–60). Because he has 'wasted time', Time itself 'doth . . . waste [destroy]' him by turning him into a 'numbering clock' (a clock telling the hours and minutes as opposed to a sundial or hourglass). His 'thoughts are minutes', moved on with sighs, his eyes the clock face, his finger the minute hand pointing always at his eyes 'in cleansing them from tears', the groans that batter at his heart the chimes that tell the hours. He has indeed become nothing more than Bullingbrook's 'Jack of the clock' (a mechanical figure that strikes the hours), who must stand and watch the days of his life go 'posting' (rushing) by.

The struggle to make sense of his situation brings Richard almost to breaking point. He angrily demands that the music be stopped before it drives him mad, yet blesses the unseen musicians, for any 'sign of love' to Richard is a 'strange brooch (rare jewel)' in such an 'all-hating world'.

As if to mark the significance of Richard's new understanding of the simple human need for love and friendship, Shakespeare introduces a brief, quiet episode demonstrating the devoted loyalty that Richard could inspire (lines 67–97). One of the grooms from his stables has with 'much ado' (difficulty) obtained permission to see him. In an attempt to comfort his 'sometime royal master', the groom tells him about Richard's favourite horse, Barbary, and how proudly he had carried the new King Henry on his back. Richard feels a momentary surge of anger that his beloved horse should have so easily switched allegiance to 'that proud man that did usurp his back', which quickly subsides when he realises that in this as in so many other matters he has only himself to blame. The horse was born to bear a burden, while he was born to rule. Yet like an ass he had permitted himself to be 'Spurred, galled [chafed] and tired by jauncing [prancing] Bullingbrook' (line 94).

The two are prevented from talking further by the entrance of Richard's 'sad dog' jailer with food. Richard clearly suspects some danger to himself and instructs the groom to leave at once. Their parting words are brief and simple, but direct and powerful (lines 96–7). When the jailer refuses to taste Richard's food to check it is not poisoned, saying that 'Sir Pierce of Exton, / Who lately came from the king' had ordered him not to, Richard's suspicions are confirmed. Behaving at last like the 'lion dying' his queen had urged him to be (Act 5 Scene 1, line 29), Richard attacks his jailer and for the first time in the play the stage erupts into violent action. The jailer's cries bring in Exton and his men, intent on murder. Desperately, Richard seizes a weapon from one of his attackers and kills at least two of them before Exton strikes him down (lines 105–7). Richard's dying words make clear to the audience the devastating consequences for the country of killing England's rightful king:

> That hand shall burn in never-quenching fire
> That staggers thus my person. Exton, thy fierce hand
> Hath with the king's blood stained the king's own land.
>
> *(lines 108–10)*

Richard's personal tragedy has run its course. In adversity, his imagination had circled ceaselessly around thoughts of failure, nothingness and the emptiness he feared might be the centre of his being. Yet in his final moments, he does truly see into his own humanity and achieve a kind of tragic dignity.

Richard's courage in the face of certain death clearly convinces Exton that the former king truly was 'of royal blood' and that his murder will be 'chronicled in hell'. Heavy with guilt, Exton prepares to take Richard on his final journey:

> This dead king to the living king I'll bear.
> Take hence the rest and give them burial here.    *(lines 117–18)*

# Act 5 Scene 6

In the previous scene, Shakespeare showed Richard finding a new strength through suffering and adversity. Now, in this final scene, he focuses on how effectively his great rival copes with governing the country. The situation at first looks ominous for Henry. Pro-Richard supporters have already set fire to the town of Ciceter (Cirencester) in Gloucestershire. The new king waits with his uncle York for further news.

Almost immediately there comes a series of favourable reports. Northumberland returns with news that he has captured and executed four of the rebel leaders and sent their heads to London (historical records state that they were set on poles over London Bridge 'to the terror of others'). Next to enter is Lord Fitzwater. Two further rebel leaders have been captured at Oxford and their heads sent to London. Fitzwater is followed by Northumberland's son, Harry Percy, who first announces that the Abbot of Westminster, 'The grand conspirator', has died and then hands over the Bishop of Carlisle to the king for judgement. King Henry, however, to demonstrate that he can be merciful as well as ruthless, spares the bishop's life on condition that he takes no further part in public life.

The scene climaxes with the entrance of Exton bearing the body of Richard in a coffin. But instead of thanking him, King Henry reacts with horror and outrage that Exton should presume to implicate him in the murder:

> Exton, I thank thee not, for thou hast wrought
> A deed of slander with thy fatal hand
> Upon my head and all this famous land.        *(lines 34–6)*

There is a strange sense of *déjà vu* about these closing moments. Just as the play began with King Richard presiding over affairs, assisted by his aged counsellor Gaunt, so it ends with Henry sitting in state with Gaunt's brother York as his adviser. Where guilt and suspicion hung over Richard concerning the death of Gloucester, a similar cloud now hangs over Henry, who shows Exton as little gratitude for carrying out his secret wishes as Richard showed to Mowbray.

Yet, despite these echoes, King Henry's 'new world' seems different – less secure, less legitimate than Richard's. Expressions of respect and allegiance to the new king are perfunctory at best.

Northumberland's greeting could be spoken in a tone of barely concealed contempt (line 6), while his son does not even make the effort to preface his news with any show of respect (lines 19–23). Neither has Henry's rule brought much-hoped-for peace and stability. New 'rebels' have appeared and authority seems to be maintained by suppression, execution, murder and blatant promises of rewards for loyalty.

Despite Exton's protests that he was only carrying out the king's wishes, Henry condemns both the man and the deed: 'They love not poison that do poison need. / Nor do I thee' (lines 38–9). But the king has much to explain and justify. In a speech full of images of blood, guilt and remorse, he banishes Exton, expresses deep sorrow and remorse at Richard's murder and asks the assembled lords to join with him in a show of mourning for the dead king:

> Lords, I protest my soul is full of woe
> That blood should sprinkle me to make me grow.
> Come mourn with me for what I do lament,
> And put on sullen black incontinent.       *(lines 45–8)*

Finally, as an act of penance, Henry vows to make a pilgrimage to the Holy Land, 'To wash this blood off' from his 'guilty hand' (line 50) before Richard's coffin is borne away with the royal court marching 'sadly after'.

This final sequence has increasingly been constructed in modern productions to raise troubling questions about Henry's sincerity and the listening lords' responses. Is Henry truly remorseful or is he feigning repentance? Do the assembled lords believe what he says or do their reactions suggest that suspicion of the new king will lead to the fresh civil discord that Shakespeare dramatises in both *King Henry IV Parts 1 and 2* (the rebellions of Northumberland and other nobles) and the three parts of *King Henry VI* (the Wars of the Roses)? At the close of the 2000 Royal Shakespeare Company production, King Henry, spotlit, held his head in his hands and wearily spoke the opening line of *King Henry IV Part 1*, 'So shaken as we are, so wan with care'.

# Act 5 Critical review

The twin journeys of the two royal cousins are drawing to a close. At his deposition, Richard compared the crown to a well with two buckets. In this final act, Shakespeare shows what Richard becomes as he descends to the depths and the price King Henry must pay for rising to the top.

As Richard struggles to come to terms with failure, the play becomes his personal tragedy. Adversity gives a new toughness to his speech as he confronts the fact that he has not just failed himself but failed his country. The imaginative and poetic powers that had once enabled him to retreat from reality are now used to accept and master it. In the darkness of his prison cell, Richard at last sees clearly. He is not just a fallen king, but a fallen man, who can never be content 'till he be eased / With being nothing'.

Loyalty becomes an even more pressing question for many characters. Since there are now two kings, which is the true king? Northumberland, York, his wife and son, Exton and even Richard's humble groom are all shown adjusting to the new regime and new loyalties.

Richard's world of glittering ceremony and feudal hierarchy has passed away. As a weary, anxious Henry IV struggles to control a darker, more sinister England, the play takes on a new tone of worldly cynicism. This 'new world' seems more 'modern', sceptical, mundane, at times almost comically undignified.

Possession of the crown brings Henry neither personal nor political peace. New rebels and new traitors threaten the safety of the crown while the conduct of his 'wanton and effeminate' son bodes ominously for its future. Henry IV, like his land, is stained with Richard's blood. The once 'bold son' of 'time-honoured' Gaunt must now bring matters to a close with guilty protestations of remorse and a vow to make penitential pilgrimage to the Holy Land.

The play therefore ends with a less than full resolution. Richard's fate may be decided, but the nation's story must go on. In the three sequel plays, Shakespeare will continue his exploration of England's history under the government of a care-worn Henry IV and his 'unthrifty son'.

## Contexts

Like every other writer, Shakespeare was influenced by many factors other than his own personal experience. The society of his time, its practices, beliefs, history and language, its political and economic affairs, culture and religion, were the raw materials on which his imagination worked.

This section identifies the contexts from which *King Richard II* emerged: the wide range of different influences which fostered the creativity of Shakespeare as he wrote the play. These contexts ensured that the play contains reminders of everyday life, and the familiar knowledge, assumptions, beliefs and values of Elizabethan England. Above all, *King Richard II* is deeply concerned with the increasingly acrimonious late sixteenth-century political debates between advocates of absolute monarchy and those who championed the right of subjects to resist a tyrannical ruler, an ideological struggle that 50 years later was to see King Charles I brought to trial by Parliament for treason, found guilty and executed.

## What did Shakespeare write?

The late sixteenth century saw a sudden rise in the popularity of historical drama. It is very probable that Shakespeare first established his reputation as a playwright with his sequence of history plays (*King Henry VI Parts 1, 2, 3* and *King Richard III*) dramatising the troubled period of fifteenth-century English history known as the Wars of the Roses. In this First Tetralogy ('sequence of four'), Shakespeare dramatises the story of England following the death of Henry V, the 'hero king'.

Following the great success of his first four history plays, Shakespeare turned his attention to events leading up to the reign of King Henry VI. *King Richard II* was probably written soon after *King Richard III* in about 1595, followed by *King Henry IV Parts 1 and 2* (1596–8) and *King Henry V* (1599). This Second Tetralogy dramatised the period of history beginning with King Richard's deposition and murder in 1399–1400, through the troubled reign of Henry IV, and ending with Henry V's famous victory against the French at Agincourt.

The two cycles of plays between them explored a period of history of enormous significance to the Elizabethans. The deposition of King Richard in 1399 by his cousin Henry Bullingbrook brought to an end a ruling dynasty which had governed England by hereditary right of succession for more than 300 years. Richard's overthrow was an act that many Elizabethans believed initiated almost 90 years of internecine dynastic conflict and civil war, interrupted only by the brief but glorious reign of Henry V. In this Elizabethan view of history, peace and stability was only ultimately secured with the overthrow of Richard III and establishment of the Tudor monarchy.

Three quarto editions of *King Richard II* were published between 1597 and 1598, all with the deposition scene in Act 4 Scene 1 removed (probably because of its politically sensitive subject matter – see pages 69–70 below). Two further quarto editions appeared in 1608 and 1615, this time with the deposition scene restored. After his death, two of Shakespeare's friends published the First Folio edition of his complete plays (1623), which grouped the works into three genre types (comedies, histories, tragedies) and placed *King Richard II* in the history section. While it is clearly a history play, many critics have commented on its qualities as tragedy: the fall of a flawed 'great man' who learns through his suffering. Some have seen in Richard an 'embryo Hamlet'. Most modern editions of the play are based on the Folio and the 1597 Quarto versions.

# What did Shakespeare read?

To prepare himself for writing what his Elizabethan audiences must have found an unsettlingly thought-provoking political-historical drama, Shakespeare seems to have been more than usually thorough and painstaking in the range and depth of material he read and absorbed.

## Tudor chroniclers

The Elizabethans' knowledge of their past was drawn largely from the many volumes of chronicle history written by Tudor scholars. These writers, however, did not always concern themselves too much with distinguishing between unsubstantiated legend and reliable evidence, since their prime purpose was to praise and justify the Tudor dynasty. They were therefore not averse to making selective use of their material for moral, didactic and propaganda purposes. Two chroniclers in particular provided Shakespeare with much of his material for *King Richard II*: Edward Hall and Raphael Holinshed.

Hall's account of the period from the deposition of King Richard II to the reign of Henry VIII was first published in 1548 and entitled *The Union of the Two Noble and Illustre Families of Lancaster and York.* Shakespeare begins *King Richard II* at exactly the same point that Hall starts his account – the quarrel between Bullingbrook and Mowbray. The pageantry of Shakespeare's Trial by Combat scene (Act 1 Scene 3) may also have been suggested by the detailed description of this event in Hall's chronicle.

Hall saw history through orthodox Tudor eyes: Bullingbrook went against God's law when he usurped the crown and murdered Richard II, for which heinous crime God punished him with rebellion and civil unrest throughout his reign. Apart from the briefly glorious reign of his son Henry V, God continued to punish England with many further decades of civil war while the families of Lancaster and York struggled for supremacy, until 'the two noble and illustre families' were once more united in the person of Henry VII, Queen Elizabeth's grandfather.

Certain elements of this 'providential' view of history figure prominently in Shakespeare's play. At Richard's deposition, for example (Act 4 Scene 1, lines 136–49), the Bishop of Carlisle prophesies that 'The blood of English shall manure the ground / And future ages groan for this foul act'. Richard's murder is presented almost as if it were a martyrdom (Act 5 Scene 5) and Henry IV, full of guilt, vows to make a pilgrimage to the Holy Land to wash the blood from his hands (Act 5 Scene 6, lines 49–50).

Shakespeare's chief source for *King Richard II* was Holinshed's *Chronicles of England, Scotlande and Irelande* (revised 1587). It contains an enormous body of information because Holinshed incorporated material from several earlier chroniclers, including Hall, into what has been described as 'one gigantic committee report'. The result was a complex mixture of often competing and contradictory accounts, both hostile and favourable to King Richard. This was just the sort of material Shakespeare needed to present a 'multi-perspective' story, where there is no clear right or wrong, but rather two competing rights.

Shakespeare does not follow Holinshed's account slavishly. As he did with all his sources, Shakespeare deepens characterisations and explores the underlying political issues. He alters events, telescopes them and changes their chronology. He adds new characters, expands the roles of existing ones and even changes their personalities. The following brief examples of how and where he diverges from his source material provide illuminating glimpses into the way he turned history into drama:

- Holinshed records that Richard was secure in Conway Castle when he was promised safe conduct under oath by Northumberland, who then laid an ambush and took him prisoner. Shakespeare's Richard, by contrast, seems to surrender to Bullingbrook, either because he wishes to or because he has no other choice – or both – an example of the play's balanced presentation of guilt and responsibility.
- Shakespeare invented the scenes with the Duchess of Gloucester (Act 1 Scene 2) and Queen Isabel (Act 2 Scene 2, Act 3 Scene 4 and Act 5 Scene 1), turning the latter (who was only a child of ten at the time) into a mature woman. The scenes with the Duchess of York are also Shakespeare's invention. Modern feminist critics have much to say about the significance of Shakespeare's inclusion of these three female figures in his play (see pages 97–9).
- Holinshed records the fact that Richard confiscated Gaunt's property, but Shakespeare creates the scene between Richard and the dying Gaunt to give the act greater 'dramatic truth', so that Richard's blatantly unjust and ultimately disastrous decision is shown to have a number of causes: to raise much needed finances, to neutralise the threat from Bullingbrook and to take angry revenge on a dying man.
- Holinshed also records that when Richard surrendered the crown (Act 4 Scene 1, line 181) he merely removed the gold signet ring from his hand and put it on Bullingbrook's finger. Shakespeare makes the moment of deposition far more dramatically complex with, for example, his haunting stage image of two crownless kings grasping the hollow crown of England.
- The 'mirror' episode in Act 4 Scene 1 is likewise Shakespeare's invention, as is Northumberland's request that Richard should publicly read out the 33 Articles listing his crimes. Richard's theatrical mirror-gazing sets up complex echoes of many of the

themes in the play: vanity, self-knowledge, appearance and reality, a king's double identity.

Simple tragic stories of great and mighty men and women from history or legend suddenly falling into poverty, despair and misery as a result of chance, accident or misfortune had been popular in England since medieval times. The stories always carried a religious moral: the benefits of this world are transitory; man's life is uncertain and we should trust only in God. The best-known example (which Shakespeare certainly read) was the popular Tudor poem *The Mirror for Magistrates* (1587). This was a collection of stories in verse about the disastrous lives of characters from history, the Bible and legend. King Richard II himself features in it, as an example of the foolishness of living and ruling by 'blind lust'.

Shakespeare may also have been influenced by Christopher Marlowe's play *King Edward II* (*c.* 1592), which also paints an initially unsympathetic portrait of a king corrupted and destroyed by his own desires.

## What was Shakespeare's England like?

Shakespeare was also strongly influenced by the many political and philosophical ideas, written about, discussed and hotly argued over in his day. Late Elizabethan England was a society in transition from a medieval to a modern age, eagerly embracing new ideas and discoveries, yet still retaining traditional beliefs and doctrines. Such a mingling of medieval and early modern worlds is very evident in *King Richard II*, where historical characters think and act in part like figures from late fourteenth-century England and in part like contemporary Elizabethans.

The opening charge of treason brought by Bullingbrook against Mowbray in the Court of Chivalry provides a good example. Both men expect to be judged not by modern process of law, but by their own medieval chivalric code of justice, where insults and accusations are first exchanged, followed by appeals to personal honour and demands for their chivalric right to personal combat. It was a practice that would have seemed strange even in Shakespeare's time. The Elizabethan nobility, however, would still have highly valued personal military prowess, even if opportunities to demonstrate it were largely confined to private duels or jousting tournaments for the entertainment of the court. (See pages 73–4 for other examples of how the play harks back to the male-dominated chivalric age of the fourteenth and fifteenth centuries.)

Many medieval medical and astrological beliefs, however, remained very much part of the Elizabethan way of life. Shakespeare's audience would have easily understood Richard's urging of Bullingbrook and Mowbray that they 'purge this choler [anger] without letting blood' because 'doctors say this is no month to bleed' (Act 1 Scene 1, lines 152–7). The medieval theory of humours believed that the healthy human body was a balanced combination of four fluids, or 'humours' (blood, choler, black bile or melancholy, and phlegm) and that human diseases and personality traits were often due to an imbalance of these humours. So, for example, an excess of choler caused angry 'choleric' behaviour, which required controlling by 'bleeding' (cutting a vein to release excess blood).

Shakespeare's England had long been a strongly Christian country, and Christian beliefs and assumptions pervade the play. Several characters refer both to devout pilgrimages and military crusades (holy wars). Bullingbrook anticipates that his fight with Mowbray will be a 'long and weary pilgrimage' (Act 1 Scene 3, line 49), Gaunt speaks of past English kings fighting for Christ as far away as Jerusalem itself and Carlisle tells how Mowbray spent his banishment fighting in the crusades (Act 4 Scene 1, lines 92–100).

In a less militaristic vein, Richard talks of exchanging jewels for a set of prayer beads, his palace for a hermitage and his sceptre for a pilgrim's walking staff (Act 3 Scene 3, lines 147–54). Several times the king portrays himself as a Christ-like martyr. Bushy, Green and Bagot betray him like 'Three Judases, each one thrice worse than Judas!' (Act 3 Scene 2, line 132), as do the entire assembly of nobles (Act 4 Scene 1, lines 170–1). Just as the Roman governor, Pontius Pilate, washed his hands of responsibility for Christ's death, so Richard sees the nobles washing their hands of responsibility for his deposition (Act 4 Scene 1, lines 236–41).

One particular aspect of Shakespeare's England that illuminates how he constructed *King Richard II* is the Elizabethan popularity for 'perspectives'. A perspective picture was a painting which disconcertingly changed its image according to the angle from which it was viewed, while a perspective glass was a piece of glass cut into a number of facets each of which created a distinct image when you looked through it. Bushy attempts to allay the queen's fears for her 'dear Richard' in Act 2 Scene 2 by using both 'perspectives' in an ingenious image (or conceit) to suggest that all her forebodings are merely tricks of the mind. The same image could equally well be applied to the complex picture Shakespeare paints of the momentous struggle between King Richard and Henry Bullingbrook. Just as a perspective painting contains more than one image, so the play's shifting and contradictory viewpoints create shifting and contradictory meanings.

What follows are some of the key features of Elizabethan life and thought that fostered Shakespeare's creativity as he wrote *King Richard II*: the dangerous world of Elizabethan politics, the conflict of ideas between the conservative doctrines of the Tudor establishment and more radical European humanist thinking, and the place of women in Elizabethan society.

## Politics

The historical King Richard II was England's supreme executive and legislative authority. He conducted day-to-day matters with advice from a small council of officials, but when matters of importance arose he would summon the nobles and bishops of England to the Great Council of Parliament, or House of Lords. There was also a second much less important body, the House of Commons, comprising representatives from the minor gentry and wealthy merchant classes – knights from country areas and wealthy burgesses from the towns. The king would only summon this body when he needed to collect the taxes he had decided to levy (Act 2 Scene 1, line 246). The great mass of the people, including the entire female population, would have been unrepresented and their wishes ignored.

To rule effectively, a king had to carry his nobles with him and persuade the Great Council of the wisdom of his policies. The most powerful barons expected to play a full part in this decision-making and were quite prepared to use their own considerable personal armies to enforce their wishes, as King Richard found to his cost in 1388 (see page 4). King Richard's reputation as a tyrant was in part due to his struggle to counter the threat of his barons' formidable private armies by building up a large permanent army of his own, a policy which forced him to employ increasingly dubious methods of raising finances (see page 15). Fear of the king's growing power and anger at his methods of extracting money created enormous resentment amongst the late fourteenth-century nobility and wealthy merchant classes. The king's seizure of Bullingbrook's inheritance was the last straw.

Queen Elizabeth's policies and style of government were much like Richard's, the key difference being that the Tudor monarchs had disbanded the aristocracy's numerous private armies and significantly curbed their powers. Where Richard's feudal government attempted and failed to establish absolute power, Elizabeth inherited and developed a more efficient administration, which usually provided sufficient resources for her to retain personal control of government policy. Her methods did not escape criticism, however, and by the late sixteenth century many of her subjects were becoming increasingly unhappy with her rule.

Many scholars have argued that Shakespeare dramatises such concerns and criticisms in *King Richard II* and that the play is a politically subversive comment on the political situation in the 1590s. Because Elizabethan theatres were subject to close censorship and could only operate if they were seen to be supportive of official authority, a dramatist could at best only make indirect comments on the pressing political issues and anxieties of his day. Open criticism of the monarch was clearly unwise, but likening Elizabeth to King Richard II offered an oblique way of expressing such concerns. Like Richard, Elizabeth was believed to be too easily led by flatterers and guilty of shedding her 'kindred blood' with the execution of her cousin, Mary Queen of Scots. Like Richard, she was childless, raising fears of civil war in disputes over the succession when she died.

Elizabeth's attempts at raising revenue to govern and keep order were strikingly similar to Richard II's and equally unpopular with the nobility, who chafed at their own diminished political influence and the queen's increasingly autocratic style of government. Queen Elizabeth herself was well aware that people were comparing her to Richard. She is recorded as remarking to her antiquary, William Lambarde, when she came upon a document concerning Richard II's reign, 'I am Richard II, know ye not that?'

Queen Elizabeth's popularity was in decline in the 1590s and support for her one-time 'favourite', the charismatic Earl of Essex, was rising. Here, yet again, there are echoes from the reign of Richard II, for Essex was a descendant of both the murdered Duke of Gloucester and the usurper Henry Bullingbrook. And on Sunday 8 February 1601 Essex likewise led a rebellion against his lawful monarch. There, however, the resemblance ends, for the attempted coup was a dismal failure and the earl was beheaded.

The story of Essex's rebellion illustrates how Shakespeare's play became dangerously involved in the world of Elizabethan politics. Some of the earl's men paid Shakespeare's company to perform a play showing 'the deposing and killing of King Richard II' on the Saturday afternoon before the Sunday rebellion. This was almost certainly Shakespeare's play. When the earl's attempted coup failed, a representative of Shakespeare's company was questioned by the authorities about their suspected involvement in the conspiracy. Fortunately no action was taken against them.

## A subject's duty of obedience

Both Church and State in Shakespeare's England tried to impress on its people that a monarch was appointed by God to rule and must therefore be obeyed. After the death of Henry VIII, special sermons ('homilies') were written by the Tudor authorities to be read in all the churches in the land (church attendance was universally required) on every Sunday and Holy Day. Queen Elizabeth I herself had a part in revising these homilies when she came to the throne. Shakespeare, like most Elizabethans, would therefore have listened many times each year to sermons on the need for order and civil obedience.

In 1571, the last and longest of these homilies, *An Homilie Against Disobedience and Wilfull Rebellion*, was published as a response to civil unrest following the abortive Northern Rebellions of the earls of Northumberland and Westmoreland. Its key message was that under no circumstances did God's law allow a subject to rebel against his monarch. In essence the homily argued for the 'Divine Right of Kings', a doctrine that the Tudor authorities had developed from earlier monarchs like King Richard II, who was said to have believed himself 'anointed by God' at his coronation. Just as God created in heaven a hierarchy of archangels and angels, so, on earth, He appointed kings and princes to rule over lords, prelates, lesser gentry, common people, 'each in their degree', a pyramid-like, hierarchical 'Chain of Being' which included birds of the air, beasts of the field, seeds, plants and trees.

Although the homily accepts that kings and princes must govern 'in authoritie, power, wisedome, providence and righteousness', it is unequivocal in its insistence that even a 'foolish', 'covetous' or 'evil' prince must be obeyed. Deposing a prince, it argues, is unthinkable, because rebellion is 'the first and principall cause, both of all worldly and bodily miseries, sorrowes, diseases, sicknesses and deathes . . . and damnation eternall'. All subjects must therefore endure with patient suffering the rule of an unjust and tyrannical prince until God sees fit to end their misery.

To what extent is a similar message to be found in *King Richard II*? Most Elizabethans had a constant fear of the return of civil war and several characters in the play warn of that danger. Richard banishes Bullingbrook and Mowbray to prevent the 'grating shock of wrathful iron arms' (Act 1 Scene 3, line 136), York accuses the returning Bullingbrook of 'Frighting [England's] pale-faced villages with war' (Act 2 Scene 3, line 93) and Bullingbrook threatens to 'lay the summer's dust with showers of blood' (Act 3 Scene 3, line 43). Perhaps the most powerful expression of orthodox Tudor belief in the play is the Bishop of Carlisle's ringing protest against the deposition of God's 'anointed' deputy and 'figure [image] of God's majesty' and his tellingly accurate prophecy that 'future ages' shall 'groan for this foul act' (Act 4 Scene 1, lines 115–49).

That does not, however, mean that the play wholeheartedly endorses a belief in the 'Divine Right of Kings'. Carlisle's mighty rhetoric does not prevent him from being arrested for 'capital treason'. Gaunt and York's refusal to act against God's 'deputy anointed' demonstrates the political paralysis that accepting such a doctrine can engender. Richard confidently claims that God will muster 'armies of pestilence' to strike down those who lift their 'vassal hands' against his crown, then almost immediately capitulates to Bullingbrook.

## New political thinking
How monarchs should govern was a frequent subject for debate in sixteenth-century Europe. One of Europe's leading Renaissance thinkers, Desiderius Erasmus of Rotterdam, in his treatise *The Education of a Christian Prince* (1516), argued that all the wars and corruption that were tearing the states of Europe apart were caused not by the rebellion of subjects but by 'foolish and tyrannical' princes (i.e. rulers). The following examples show how Shakespeare persistently echoes similar ideas in *King Richard II*:

- Erasmus argued that only princes of the highest moral integrity, who put the interests of state before their own pleasures, are fit to govern. The rest are sham princes, mere actors decked out with symbolic regalia. Critics have often commented on Richard's theatrical behaviour, not least his masterly management of his own deposition.
- A prince must exercise proper management of his own body and soul, and like a doctor watch over the body of his kingdom, for 'what is the prince but the physician of the state?' Richard is several times criticised for failing to do this. Gaunt, for example, accuses him of causing the moral sickness both of himself and of his country (Act 2 Scene 1, lines 91–103).
- God will judge the mighty far more severely than other men, because their power and wealth should be a burden 'which they bear for others rather than for themselves'. In Pomfret prison, Richard likewise muses upon the fate of kings and how hard it is for a rich man to enter the kingdom of heaven (Act 5 Scene 5, lines 15–38).
- Erasmus stopped short of advocating forcible deposition of an evil prince, but did argue that such a man should 'yield' his authority to one more fit for royal office. That Shakespeare's Richard voluntarily resigned his crown to Bullingbrook is mentioned several times in *King Richard II* (something significantly absent from Shakespeare's sources).

Some Renaissance writers, however, *were* willing to countenance the deposition of a Prince. Traditional Tudor belief was that a king's immortal 'royal' body was fused together with his physical body at the moment of coronation (a concept known as 'The King's Two Bodies') and transferred to his successor upon the death of his mortal one. These two bodies were believed to fuse together at the moment of coronation, rather as the immortal being of Christ was fused with his mortal body at his incarnation.

More radical thinkers took this concept a stage further. They argued that if a king's immortal body could be transferred on the death of his natural body why could it not also be transferred *before* death, should that monarch prove a tyrant? Shakespeare's play may also sometimes question orthodox Tudor arguments in support of absolute monarchy, but does it unequivocally advocate the need to resist monarchical power? Again the answer, as Richard might say, is 'aye – no', because, significantly, Shakespeare has the most unambiguous call for the lords to 'shake off' their 'slavish yoke' issue from the mouth of Northumberland, perhaps the most ruthlessly self-seeking character in the play (Act 2 Scene 1, line 291).

Niccolò Machiavelli of Florence, in his handbook for rulers, *The Prince* (1532), preaches a very different message from Erasmus. If Erasmus wrote about how rulers *ought* to govern, Machiavelli wrote about how they *did* govern. In a wicked world, he argued, it is perfectly justifiable for princes to use any means, however unethical or immoral, to stay in power and he offered a series of ruthless and manipulative instructions for ensuring that they would never be overthrown. Many Elizabethans criticised Machiavelli publicly for his cynical advocacy of murder and treachery, but studied him in private for his rigorously practical approach to government.

There is perhaps something of the machiavel (villainous plotter and schemer) in Shakespeare's portrait of the Earl of Northumberland, as he turns the discontented lords against Richard (Act 2 Scene 1, lines 224–300), before obsequiously manoeuvring himself into Bullingbrook's good favour (Act 2 Scene 3, lines 2–18). Both Richard and Bullingbrook show some of Machiavelli's ruthlessness. Richard probably had his uncle Gloucester murdered, banished his cousin Bullingbrook and seized Gaunt's lands and property. Bullingbrook is careful to reveal little of his true intentions in the play, cynically courts popularity with the people and has Richard murdered. The Gardener, however, is perhaps the most machiavellian of all. King Richard should quite simply have 'like an executioner / Cut off the heads of too-fast-growing' lords 'That look too lofty in our commonwealth' (Act 3 Scene 4, lines 33–5).

## A golden age of heroes

Queen Elizabeth I presided over an exclusively male world of politics and government, where many questioned a woman's ability to rule. They disliked what they saw as the decadence and effeminacy of her court with its new breed of politicians and administrators. In their dissatisfaction, they looked back nostalgically to fourteenth- and fifteenth-century England as a golden age of male militaristic and chivalric values.

There is a similar sense of dissatisfaction and a nostalgia for a past (equally mythical) Golden Age in the opening acts of *King Richard II* where one figure after another accuses the king of betraying England's heroic male heritage. Most famously, the dying Gaunt remembers his England as 'This royal throne of kings', 'this seat of Mars', 'This fortress', and the English as 'This happy breed of men' feared and famous throughout the known world for their military exploits and 'true chivalry' (Act 2 Scene 1, lines 31–68). Other disgruntled nobles recall with approval the legendary era of King Edward III and his seven sons.

Just as some Elizabethans compared Queen Elizabeth unfavourably to her father Henry VIII and criticised her for her reluctance to go to war, so Shakespeare's Richard is shown to be overshadowed by his father. After the death of Gaunt (Act 2 Scene 1, lines 171–85), York makes it abundantly clear that Richard may look like his famous father but certainly does not act like him. The Black Prince 'frowned' against the French, York says, and not against his friends, gaining his wealth in foreign wars, not wasting what his ancestors had fought for, spilling his enemies' blood and not his own family's.

## Women in Elizabethan society

Elizabethan politics, with the notable exception of the queen herself, was an almost exclusively male domain. English history as recorded by the Tudor chroniclers was likewise exclusively masculine – written by men about men. A glance at the cast list for *King Richard II* would seem to indicate that Shakespeare reflected this gender imbalance. Of the 30 or more named characters in *King Richard II*, there are only three female roles of any significance: Queen Isabel and the Duchesses of Gloucester and York. All three, as wife or mother, depend for their identity upon the status of their husband. All three are on the margins of history – even the Gardener is better informed about events than the queen. All seem born to grieve and suffer, reduced to pleading or cajoling with male authority. The Duchess of Gloucester cannot revenge her husband's murder without Gaunt's help (Act 1 Scene 2) and Queen Isabel must beg her defeated and demoralised husband to behave more like 'the king of beasts' (Act 5 Scene 1). Both fail. The Duchess of York, although more active in her son's defence, must still flatter and plead with male authority, mocked by her husband as a 'frantic woman' whose 'old dugs [breasts]' have reared a traitor (Act 5 Scene 3, lines 88–9).

Yet some critics have argued that Shakespeare does not merely present these marginal female roles as natural and inevitable, but rather uses their predicament to question the justice of a society that should treat women in such a way. In the 1590s, traditional assumptions of male superiority were beginning to be questioned and women, at least in the capital, often enjoyed a degree of freedom. In particular, there was Queen Elizabeth herself: highly intelligent and educated, fluent in several languages and a skilful politician, who governed the country for 45 years and kept England safe from invasion and civil war.

The despair and sorrow of Shakespeare's Duchess of Gloucester is born out of frustration and impotence. She has the male warrior's thirst for battle, reproaching Gaunt for his 'pale cold cowardice' and longing for the moment when Bullingbrook's spear shall 'enter butcher Mowbray's breast' (Act 1 Scene 2, line 48). But a male-dominated society which values military prowess above all else ensures that she can never take matters into her own hands. The aged Duchess of York shows something of a 'man's' physical courage, riding 'as fast as York' to save her son, but she fights for 'female' virtues of mercy and forgiveness. Her actions successfully question her 'hard-hearted' lord's male belief that allegiance to your king must come before love for your son. She wins her husband over ('Thine eye begins to speak' Act 5 Scene 3, line 124) and the king is merciful. Modern feminist/historicist critics have shown particular interest in how the play's female characters challenge rather than reinforce the play's masculine, military values (see pages 97–9).

# Language

Contrary to the popular belief that he was a 'natural writer', utterly spontaneous, inspired only by his imagination, Shakespeare had a profound knowledge of the language techniques of his own and previous times, particularly rhetoric. Rhetoric is the study of the various linguistic effects which writers and speakers employ to make their language persuasive, memorable or moving. It is a skill which Shakespeare uses to the full in *King Richard II*. The play is full of set speeches written in a consistently elevated and stylised manner: angry accusations and denials, statesmanlike declarations of policy, denunciations and chilling prophecies of disaster, ritualistic and quasi-religious ceremonies, philosophical meditations and grief-stricken laments. Even low-ranking characters such as the Welsh Captain and the Gardener speak with fluency and control, as if they were members of an ancient Greek chorus commenting on the tragic events taking place around them.

What follows is an analysis of some of the language techniques Shakespeare uses in *King Richard II* to intensify dramatic effect, create mood and character, and so produce memorable theatre. As you read the play, always keep in mind that Shakespeare wrote for theatre-goers, not readers. Elizabethan dramatic language, because written to be heard, tends to be more patterned, with distinctive rhythms and repetitions of words and phrases to help the audience keep track of what the actor is saying.

## Imagery

*King Richard II* abounds in imagery (sometimes called 'figurative language'): vivid words and phrases that help create the atmosphere of the play as they conjure up emotionally charged mental pictures or associations in the imagination. In the opening scene, for example, the nobility's pride in their aristocratic status, military prowess and chivalric honour is powerfully expressed in images of anger, aggression and killing, spears, swords and lances, the swearing of oaths and hurling down of gages (gauntlets) in challenge to mortal combat.

Early critics such as John Dryden and Doctor Johnson were critical of Shakespeare's fondness for imagery. They felt that many images obscured meaning and detracted attention from the subjects they represented. Over the past two hundred years, however, critics, poets and audiences have increasingly valued Shakespeare's imagery. They recognise how he uses it to give pleasure as it stirs the audience's imagination, deepens the dramatic impact of particular moments or moods, provides insight into character, and intensifies meaning and emotional force. Images can carry powerful significance far deeper than their surface meanings.

Shakespeare's Elizabethan world provides much of the play's imagery. Northumberland likens the nobility's lack of action in the face of growing monarchical crisis to a ship which sees the 'fearful tempest' approach but refuses to 'strike' (furl) its sails to weather out the storm (Act 2 Scene 1, lines 263–6), then urges the lords to 'Imp out' (repair) their 'drooping country's broken wing', a term taken from the aristocratic sport of falconry (line 292). In medieval times it was generally thought that the earth was the centre of the universe and that the sun, planets and stars all revolved around it, a belief that was not really challenged until well into the sixteenth century. It is an idea that Richard uses in Act 3 Scene 2, lines 36–53 to describe the impact his return from Ireland will have on Bullingbrook, when, like the sun, he rises up 'from under this terrestrial ball' to expose the traitor to 'the sight of day'.

Shakespeare's imagery employs metaphor, simile and personification. All are comparisons that, in effect, substitute one thing (the image) for another (the thing described).

- A *simile* compares one thing to another using 'like' or 'as'. The duration of a Trial by Combat was from dawn to dusk, so before their battle Bullingbrook describes himself and Mowbray as 'like two men / That vow a long and weary pilgrimage' (Act 1 Scene 3, lines 48–9). Salisbury foresees Richard's glory falling 'like a shooting star' (Act 2 Scene 4, line 19).
- A *metaphor* is also a comparison. It does not use 'like' or 'as', but suggests that two dissimilar things are actually the same. Gaunt's famous protest at his country's decline under Richard's rule (Act 2 Scene 1, lines 40–60) uses a series of resonantly powerful metaphors to express how great England used to be: 'This royal throne of kings, this sceptred isle', 'this seat of Mars', 'This other

Eden, demi-paradise', 'This precious stone set in the silver sea', 'This nurse, this teeming womb of royal kings'.

- *Personification* turns all kinds of things into persons, giving them human feelings or attributes. The aged Gaunt knows that 'blindfold Death' will prevent him from seeing his son return from banishment (Act 1 Scene 3, line 223). Faced with an increasingly erratic and tyrannical king, Northumberland offers hope to Ross and Willoughby by describing how 'Even through the hollow eyes of death' he can 'spy life peering' (Act 2 Scene 1, lines 270–1).

A particular type of imagery which recurs in the play is the *conceit* (an extended or far-fetched image in which a very unlikely connection between two things is established). Such fanciful comparisons, like Bushy's likening of the queen's fears to a perspective painting (see page 22), seem odd at first, but on reflection reveal a kind of truth. It is as if their strange complexity reflects the complexity of life itself. Richard fittingly speaks the play's most memorable conceits, seduced into figurative flights of imagination even in the most desperate of situations: describing the antic Death keeping court 'within the hollow crown / That rounds the mortal temples of a king' (Act 3 Scene 2, lines 160–1); imagining himself and Aumerle digging their own graves with tears (Act 3 Scene 3, lines 161–9); filling his prison with thought-people and likening himself to a mechanical clock (Act 5 Scene 5, lines 1–60).

In *King Richard II* Shakespeare weaves a whole series of linked and interrelated themes and images together: earth, air, fire and water; blood, anger, kinship and murder; melancholy, tears and weeping; beggary and bankruptcy; tongues and names; gardens and growing; hollowness and shadows; plague, pestilence and infection. Particular image-themes appear periodically through the play, but much more insistently at crucial moments. The following examples show something of the complexity of this 'tapestry' of images.

## Elemental imagery

The critic Andrew Gurr declares of the play that 'Fire and water struggle for the earth of England and conduct their fight with the airy breath of words.' Medieval and Elizabethan belief was that the four elements of earth, air, fire and water made up the entire world. Fire (hot and dry) and air (warm and moist) were both upwardly aspiring, while earth (cool and dry) and water (cold and wet) both tended downwards. Shakespeare organises many of the images in the play around this notion that the four elements were always contrary to or in permanent conflict with each other and by their very nature in constant movement either up or down. Elemental images are again particularly evident in the opening scene. Bullingbrook and Mowbray are 'In rage deaf as the sea, hasty as fire' (line 19). Mowbray is an ugly cloud in a 'fair and crystal' sky (line 41). The murdered Gloucester is imagined crying out for vengeance 'Even from the tongueless caverns of the earth' (line 105). When Richard sardonically remarks of Bullingbrook 'How high a pitch his resolution soars!' (line 109), he combines both height and air in his image of his cousin's hawk-like ambition.

It is, however, in the play's central scenes (Act 3 Scenes 2 and 3) that elemental images feature most strongly, as Richard the sun-king struggles against Bullingbrook the flood. Returned from Ireland, Richard confidently imagines himself rising like the sun in the east to expose Bullingbrook's treason, confident in his belief that neither 'the rough rude sea' nor 'breath of worldly men' can take away his right to rule England (Act 3 Scene 2, lines 54–7). But then Salisbury reports how the king's return has been 'clouded' by the dispersal of his Welsh army (lines 67–74) and Scroope likens Bullingbrook's growing power to a swelling silver river covering Richard's 'fearful land' (lines 106–11). The scene ends with Richard in despair. No longer the sun-king, he forbids anyone to wound him 'with the flatteries of his tongue', ordering his followers to 'hence away / From Richard's night to Bullingbrook's fair day' (lines 217–18).

Before Flint Castle, Bullingbrook himself anticipates that the momentous confrontation with Richard will be as terrifying as the 'thundering shock' when 'the elements / Of fire and water' meet and tear apart 'the cloudy cheeks of heaven' (Act 3 Scene 3, lines 54–7). When Richard appears on the castle walls Bullingbrook compares him to the 'blushing discontented sun / . . . / When he perceives the envious clouds are bent / To dim his glory' (lines 63–6). When Richard learns that Bullingbrook requires him to descend to 'the base court' to meet him, he compares himself to 'glistering Phaëton', son of Apollo the sun god (see page 36).

## Blood imagery
Blood images, with their additional connotations of kinship and killing, predominate in the early exchanges between Mowbray,

Bullingbrook and Richard (Act 1 Scene 1): 'full of ire', 'The blood is hot', 'high blood's royalty', 'streams of blood', 'slander of his blood', 'sacred blood', 'best blood', 'without letting blood', 'no month to bleed', 'heart blood'.

Other blood images appear through the remainder of the play in varying forms: Gaunt chases 'the royal blood / With fury' from Richard's face (Act 2 Scene 1, lines 118–19), accusing him of drunkenly carousing, like the pelican, on his own uncle's blood (lines 126–7). The Welsh Captain fears to see 'The pale faced moon' look 'bloody on the earth' (Act 2 Scene 4, line 10). Bullingbrook conducts a public trial of Bushy and Green 'to wash [the] blood / From off [his] hands' (Act 3 Scene 1, lines 5–6).

At the moment of crisis in Act 3 Scene 2, 'the blood of twenty thousand men' drains from Richard's face (line 76); later Bullingbrook threatens to 'lay the summer's dust with showers of blood' (Act 3 Scene 3, line 43) and Richard warns that rebellion will cost 'Ten thousand bloody crowns of mothers' sons' (line 96).

Blood images also feature significantly in the final scenes. Richard tells Exton that his 'fierce hand' has 'with the king's blood stained the king's own land'. When King Henry hears of Richard's murder, he protests deep sorrow that 'blood should sprinkle' him to make him grow and vows to make a pilgrimage to the Holy Land to 'wash this blood' from his 'guilty hand'.

## Hollowness and crowns

The Duchess of Gloucester is one of the first to talk of 'empty hollowness' (Act 1 Scene 2, line 59). In subsequent scenes, Aumerle refers to his 'hollow parting' from Bullingbrook (Act 1 Scene 4, line 9), Gaunt speaks of the grave 'Whose hollow womb inherits naught but bones', and Northumberland speaks of 'the hollow eyes of death' (Act 2 Scene 1, lines 83 and 270).

Richard uses his own crown in the deposition scene to suggest how transitory a king's hold on power can be by comparing it to a deep well with two buckets in which sit himself and Bullingbrook. Other crown images in the play also focus on how precarious a king's position can be. Gaunt tells Richard 'A thousand flatterers sit within thy crown' (Act 2 Scene 1, line 100) and Richard instructs Northumberland to tell Bullingbrook that the crown he seeks will be paid for with 'Ten thousand bloody crowns of mothers' sons' (Act 3 Scene 3, line 96).

The two image-themes of crowns and hollowness come together most intensely when events bring home to Richard how much his royal power has ebbed away. Scroope's description of the king's advisers lying 'full low, graved in the hollow ground' prompts Richard to muse on the hollowness of life where all we can hope to call our own is 'that small model of the barren earth / Which serves as paste and cover to our bones' and how 'within the hollow crown / That rounds the mortal temples of a king / Keeps Death his court' (Act 3 Scene 2, lines 140, 153–4 and 160–2).

## Faces and shadows

The historical Richard was notorious for outbursts of rage, which would leave his cheeks either flushed or pale, a fact which Shakespeare twice uses in the play: at Gaunt's criticisms (Act 2 Scene 1, lines 118–19) and again at news of the dispersal of his Welsh army (Act 3 Scene 2, lines 75–9). The earliest face image, however, is Bullingbrook's threat to spit his own tongue bleeding 'even in Mowbray's face' (Act 1 Scene 1, line 195).

York tells Richard he has his father's face (Act 2 Scene 1, line 176) and accuses Bullingbrook of frightening England's 'pale-faced villages with war' (Act 2 Scene 3, line 93), a phrase which is echoed by Richard in his image of the 'flower of England's face' (Act 3 Scene 3, line 97). The Welsh Captain sees how 'The pale faced moon looks bloody on the earth' (Act 2 Scene 4, line 10) and Richard imagines how Bullingbrook's 'treasons will sit blushing in his face' (Act 3 Scene 2, line 51).

Shadow images are used by Bushy to comfort the queen, when he says how any one grief will have 'twenty shadows' and assures her that her fears are really 'naught but shadows' (Act 2 Scene 2, lines 14 and 23).

Both face and shadow images are powerfully brought together by Shakespeare in the climactic moment of the deposition scene (Act 4 Scene 1). Richard calls for a mirror to see if anything yet remains of his former majesty, then smashes the glass, declaring 'Mark, silent king, the moral of this sport, / How soon my sorrow hath destroyed my face.' This provokes the hitherto controlled and silent Bullingbrook to respond:

> The shadow of your sorrow hath destroyed
> The shadow of your face.          *(Act 4 Scene 1, lines 291–2)*

## Gardens

England is many times compared to a garden or farm that requires careful tending, using images of planting and harvesting, weeding, ploughing and manuring, pruning, grafting and lopping. Gaunt speaks of 'This other Eden', 'This blessed plot', which Richard in his folly has turned into a worthless smallholding or 'pelting farm' (Act 2 Scene 1, line 60). Bullingbrook refers to Richard's advisers as 'The caterpillars of the commonwealth', which he will 'weed and pluck away' (Act 2 Scene 3, lines 165–6), and the Welsh Captain speaks of bay trees withering (Act 2 Scene 4, line 8).

At the heart of the play is the scene in York's garden where the gardeners view with dismay their 'sea-wallèd garden, the whole land' full of weeds, unpruned trees and 'wholesome herbs / Swarming with caterpillars' and condemn King Richard for not having tended to his realm in the way that they have 'trimmed and dressed' their garden (Act 3 Scene 4, lines 43–7 and 55–7).

## Language, thought and reality

Language is yet another significant image-theme which is present in the play from the opening scene. Words like 'tongue', 'word', 'breath', 'throat', 'air' and 'name' occur repeatedly throughout the play. Characters speak with public confidence, but it is often hard to know if what they say is what they mean. Bullingbrook and Mowbray at first address their 'gracious sovereign' with commendable respect, but at least one of them is lying, as Richard sardonically observes (Act 1 Scene 1, lines 20–7). If some hide behind their words, others use them to manipulate others or deceive themselves. Each character has their own vision of the truth. The Duchess of Gloucester believes her husband's death was butchery, while the Gardener calls it necessary pruning.

Bullingbrook claims to see his words as linked firmly and unambiguously to his actions. Reality should dominate language and thought. 'What my tongue speaks my right drawn sword may prove', he insists, and later claims that if his tongue were ever to 'wound [his] honour' by speaking something he did not mean, he would tear it from his mouth (Act 1 Scene 1, lines 46 and 190–5). When Gaunt urges him to use the power of words to turn his bitter banishment into a journey of delight, his son is forthright in his dismissal of such foolishness:

> Oh, who can hold a fire in his hand
> By thinking on the frosty Caucasus?
>
> *(Act 1 Scene 3, lines 293–4)*

Words, however, hold a fatal fascination for Richard. At the height of his power, he seems to believe he can say and do exactly as he wants, because the king's word will create whatever reality the king desires, a claim that even Bullingbrook sardonically concedes when Richard arbitrarily removes four years from his term of banishment (Act 1 Scene 3, lines 212–14). But Richard's faith in the power of the king's word is a delusion. News of Bullingbrook's return to England does not at first shake Richard's confidence that his sun-like majesty as 'an anointed king', aided by God's 'glorious' angels, will overcome the rebels (Act 3 Scene 2, lines 6–62). Richard's sensitivity to words and images at times lures him into passive acceptance of defeat, such as when Northumberland's request for the king to descend to the 'base court' becomes in Richard's mind an anguished premonition of his imminent loss of kingship (Act 3 Scene 3, lines 176–83). It is as though Richard looks to language to give him his identity and fears that without the name of king he will be nothing:

> I have no name, no title,
> No, not that name was given me at the font,
> But 'tis usurped. Alack the heavy day
> That I have worn so many winters out
> And know not now what name to call myself.
>
> *(Act 4 Scene 1, lines 254–8)*

## Antithesis

Antithesis is the opposition of words or phrases against each other, as when for example the anguished Richard realises his world has been overturned and Bullingbrook is now the master: 'For night owls shriek where mounting larks should sing'. This setting of word/phrase/image against word/phrase/image ('night owls shriek' stands in contrast to 'mounting larks should sing') is one of Shakespeare's favourite language devices. The phrase 'set(s) the word itself against the word' appears twice in *King Richard II* (Act 5 Scene 3, line 121 and Scene 5, lines 13–14).

Shakespeare uses antithesis extensively in all his plays, because it powerfully expresses conflict through its use of opposites, and conflict is the essence of all drama. He sets character against character, scene against scene, emotional tone against emotional tone, phrase against phrase, word against word. This concern for comparison and contrast, opposition and juxtaposition is frequently seen in the imagery of *King Richard II*, with its complex interweaving of opposing and contrary images (fire and air are set against earth and water; there are images of balancing scales and of buckets going up and down in a well).

Antithesis also occurs in other ways. Gaunt, for example, uses it to urge his son to fight the pain of banishment: 'Think not the king did banish thee, / But thou the king' (Act 1 Scene 3, lines 278–9). Richard leaves to visit the dying Gaunt with the callously witty, 'Pray God we may make haste and come too late' (Act 1 Scene 4, line 63), and answers York's assurances of both Gaunt and Bullingbrook's loyalty with this enigmatic antithesis:

> Right, you say true. As Herford's love, so his.
> As theirs, so mine, and all be as it is.
>
> *(Act 2 Scene 1, lines 145–6)*

## Repetition

Different forms of language repetition run through the play, contributing to its atmosphere, creation of character and dramatic force. The recurring patterns of words and images such as earth, air, fire, water, blood, tears, gardens, sweet and sour have already been discussed, and Shakespeare uses repetition in other ways.

Repeated words, phrases, rhythms and sounds add intensity to the moment or episode. They can heighten theatrical effect and deepen emotional and imaginative significance. When Richard greets his uncle with a cheery 'What comfort, man? How is't with agèd Gaunt?', the dying man plays bitterly and repeatedly with his own name: 'Old Gaunt indeed, and gaunt in being old.' Concern for the state of the country and grief at his son's absence have indeed made him gaunt:

> Gaunt am I for the grave, gaunt as a grave,
> Whose hollow womb inherits naught but bones.
>
> *(Act 2 Scene 1, lines 82–3)*

# Lists

One of Shakespeare's favourite language methods is to accumulate words or phrases rather like a list, intensifying and varying description, atmosphere and argument as he 'piles up' item on item, incident on incident. Every list in *King Richard II* has a particular dramatic purpose. The way Northumberland presents the leading figures in Bullingbrook's tiny invasion force of just eight ships and 3,000 men, for example, is designed to create a sense of mounting excitement and make the rebels seem more formidable than they really are (Act 2 Scene 1, lines 277–90).

After stopping the Trial by Combat, Richard delays revealing his judgement until he has slowly and solemnly listed the compelling reasons for ending Bullingbrook and Mowbray's 'rival-hating envy', thus ensuring that the actual decision hits home with maximum impact: 'Therefore we banish you our territories' (Act 1 Scene 3, lines 125–39). In the deposition scene, the Bishop of Carlisle first ringingly lists the many ways in which Richard's god-like authority has been described, to stress the enormity of what the assembled nobles are about to do (Act 4 Scene 1, lines 125–9), then lists the horrors that will be visited upon the country if Bullingbrook is crowned king (Act 4 Scene 1, lines 137–44).

# Puns

A pun is a play on words where the writer exploits a word's ambiguity (double meaning) or its similarity in sound to another word. Shakespeare often uses puns in his plays for comic effect, but in *King Richard II* their purpose is deadly serious, as Gaunt's repeated playing on the meaning of his own name demonstrates (see above, page 84), or when York admonishes Northumberland for omitting King Richard's title (Act 3 Scene 3, lines 7–17). Bullingbrook begs his uncle not to 'mistake' (misunderstand, take amiss) what Northumberland says, but York's reply plays on another possible meaning of 'mistake' (i.e. mis-take or take illegally) to warn his nephew of the dangers of taking more than is rightfully his.

Richard, of course, is most given to this kind of wordplay. Even as he hands over the symbols of power, his words have a double edge as he says 'Now, mark me how I will undo [undress or destroy] myself' (Act 4 Scene 1, line 202). Later in the same scene, as he looks in the mirror, he asks himself, 'Is this the face which faced [covered up, condoned] so many follies, / That was at last outfaced [overcome] by Bullingbrook?' (lines 284–5). Then when Bullingbrook gives instructions to 'convey [escort] him to the Tower', Richard uses the word 'convey' with its two other meanings ('to transfer the title to property' and 'to steal') to accuse the entire assembly of stealing his crown (lines 316–17): 'Conveyers are you all / That rise thus nimbly by a true king's fall.'

## Verse

*King Richard II* is written entirely in verse. This is very much in keeping with the formal and ceremonial style with which Shakespeare presents the momentous political events of Richard's deposition, so that even his lowest ranking characters, like the Groom, Gardener, Captain and Keeper (prison guard), speak in measured verse. Critics have often commented on the poetic and lyrical qualities of the play, as if through its highly patterned language Shakespeare were attempting to embody his own vision of a past medieval world.

About 80 per cent of the play is in blank verse (unrhymed verse written in iambic pentameter): the standard verse form for all of Shakespeare's plays. In Greek, *penta* means 'five' and *iamb* means a 'foot' of two syllables, the first unstressed and the second stressed. Iambic pentameter is therefore a metre in which each line has five alternating stressed (/) and unstressed (×) syllables, as in Gaunt's famous line:

> × / × / × / × / × /
> This royal throne of kings, this sceptred isle
>
> *(Act 2 Scene 1, line 40)*

Regular blank verse tends to pause at the end of each line ('end-stopping') and to have a mid-line pause (*caesura*). These features are frequently used by Shakespeare to convey the balances and contrasts in the play, such as when Richard hands over power to Bullingbrook:

> With mine own tears I wash away my balm;
> With mine own hands I give away my crown;
> With mine own tongue deny my sacred state;
> With mine own breath release all duteous oaths.
>
> *(Act 4 Scene 1, lines 206–9)*

Alternatively, one verse line can 'flow' into the next (*enjambement* or 'run-on line'), as in Richard's affirmation:

> For every man that Bullingbrook hath pressed
> To lift shrewd steel against our golden crown
> God for His Richard hath in heavenly pay
> A glorious angel.                    *(Act 3 Scene 2, lines 58–61)*

Shakespeare achieves his effects by the way he rings the changes on these rhythmic patterns. The blank verse structure sets up a rhythmic pattern and energy, and when that basic rhythm is changed or broken, other often quite striking effects are created. One such moment is when Richard finally agrees to resign the crown. After a series of regularly patterned lines, where Richard muses on 'loss of care' and 'gain of care', Bullingbrook asks him directly if he is 'contented to resign the crown'. The momentary broken rhythm of Richard's answer exactly captures his mixture of desire and reluctance:

> / / /  / × / ×  / × /
> Aye – no. No – aye, for I must nothing be
> *(Act 4 Scene 1, lines 200–1)*

### Rhyming couplets

About one fifth of the play is in rhyming verse, mostly couplets (pairs of rhyming lines). Their basic use can be clearly seen in the opening scene, where the first couplet employed neatly expresses Richard's anticipation of a stormy encounter with the two Lords Appellant:

> High stomached are they both and full of ire,
> In rage deaf as the sea, hasty as fire.
> *(Act 1 Scene 1, lines 18–19)*

Couplets are often used by Shakespeare to create a strong conclusion to a character's statement (e.g. Act 1 Scene 1, lines 41–6), or to mark the end of a scene or exit of a character, such as the dying Gaunt's angry couplet as he is carried off stage and the petulant riposte that Richard hurls after him (Act 2 Scene 1, lines 137–40).

Examples abound elsewhere in the play of rhyming couplets used for a wide variety of effects. Richard's despair at the end of Act 3

Scene 2 is expressed in a sequence of five couplets, which not even Aumerle's interruption can break. The couplet form holds the queen's 'nameless' fears together (Act 2 Scene 2, lines 31–2); in a later scene, the Gardener is moved by the queen's grief-stricken couplets to respond in like manner (Act 3 Scene 4, lines 96–107); Aumerle's machiavellian advice to Richard is delivered in a succinct couplet (Act 3 Scene 3, lines 131–2), as is Richard's callously trite response to the news of Gaunt's death (Act 2 Scene 1, lines 153–4). Perhaps the most surprising sequence of couplets, however, is in Act 5 Scene 3, where the Duchess of York's entrance sets off a long series of couplets of a comic knockabout quality rarely seen elsewhere in the play, as King Henry himself observes:

> Our scene is altered from a serious thing,
> And now changed to 'The Beggar and the King'.
>
> *(Act 5 Scene 3, lines 78–9)*

## Stichomythia

This is the most highly patterned formal verse to be found in the play. It is a form of rhymed verse dialogue, originally from Greek drama, in which single lines are spoken by alternate characters. Such dialogue is both strongly repetitive and antithetical, as each speaker takes up and echoes the other's words. Elizabethan dramatists often employed it in situations where there was some argument or difference between two people.

Shakespeare first uses stichomythia to present the awkwardly formal leave-taking between Bullingbrook and his father (Act 1 Scene 3, lines 257–62) and then to show the hitherto loyal Gaunt's anger at Richard's stewardship of his realm (Act 2 Scene 1, lines 84–94). There is an interesting variation on this pattern in Richard's farewell to his queen, where Shakespeare has them joined by Northumberland, as if it were an operatic aria for tenor, soprano and villainous bass (Act 5 Scene 1, lines 81–6).

# Critical approaches

The value of looking at criticism from different historical periods is the range of perspectives which it throws on a text and how to read it. *King Richard II* has an intriguing critical history and responses to it over the centuries have been fierce and often contradictory.

When first performed, the play was politically controversial because it showed on stage the deposition of a king and it continued to be politically significant throughout most of the seventeenth century. But by the eighteenth century, as the monarchy lost its central position of power in the British political system, so interest in the play waned and it was rarely produced on stage. Its popularity revived in the nineteenth century, although critics were now more concerned with the personal tragedy of Richard than with questions of monarchical power. Intensive study of the play began only in the twentieth century and by the 1940s it had become one of Shakespeare's most popular plays, particularly influenced by E M W Tillyard's critical readings of the history plays. With Tillyard, attention once again focused on *King Richard II*'s political significance, but the play was now seen as essentially supportive of the Tudor status quo rather than questioning and subversive. Criticism since Tillyard has often been concerned with challenging his conservative stance, arguing that other more ambiguous and dissenting voices are to be heard in the play. Since 1970, the new models of critical thinking such as new historicism, cultural materialism, feminism, psychoanalysis and postmodernism, have each offered significantly different readings of the play.

## Traditional criticism

The first substantial critical assessments of *King Richard II* appeared in the latter part of the seventeenth century. John Dryden (1679) was particularly moved by York's description of the deposed Richard being led in triumph through the streets of London: 'consider the wretchedness of his condition and his carriage [demeanour] in it; and refrain from pity if you can'. In 1680, Nahum Tate felt obliged to write an 'improved' version of *King Richard II* and the comments he makes in his preface reveal what he thought of the original. He is unhappy, for example, with the way Shakespeare presents his characters with faults as well as virtues. Richard especially should behave in a nobly heroic fashion and his motives be clearly above suspicion.

A century of critical neglect followed, during which even Samuel Johnson, usually a stout defender of Shakespeare's plays, could find little in *King Richard II* 'to affect the passions or enlarge the understanding' (1765). Interest in the play, however, began to revive in the nineteenth century. Wilhelm Schlegel (1767–1845), a German scholar, was the first critic to see an epic design to Shakespeare's whole cycle of English history plays. His vision of the plays as a single unit concerned with the theme of kingship and the curse that fell on England after Richard's deposition is a forerunner of many twentieth-century interpretations.

The primary concern of nineteenth-century English critics was with character – in particular with the 'inner emotional life' of Richard, about which there was considerable disagreement. Samuel Taylor Coleridge (1813) regarded Richard as unfit for kingship because he was 'weak, womanish, variable', yet found him, for all his faults, a sympathetic figure. William Hazlitt (1817) echoes Coleridge's description of Richard as a 'weak king', but is more judgemental. Richard bewails his loss of kingly power, but does nothing to prevent it and allows himself to be crushed and trampled 'under insults and injuries, which his own misconduct had provoked, but which he has not courage nor manliness to resent . . . We feel neither respect nor love for the deposed monarch; for he is as wanting in energy as in principle: but we pity him, for he pities himself.'

Later nineteenth-century critics were equally divided over their interpretation of Richard's character. Edward Dowden (1875) writes about the king as if he were moralising about a real person rather than a dramatic construct. Richard is 'without true kingly strength or dignity', the implication being that he would have benefited from a good dose of Victorian manliness, self-discipline and moral fibre. Walter Pater's views (1889), however, contrast strongly with Dowden's deeply unsympathetic portrait. For Pater, Richard is the most 'sweet-tongued' of Shakespeare's kings, 'an exquisite poet if he is nothing else, from first to last, in light and gloom alike, able to see things poetically'. More significantly, Pater sees Richard the poet-king as only one element in the play's overall dramatic form, which he compares to 'a musical composition' with 'something like the unity of a lyrical ballad, a lyric, a song, a single strain of music'.

A significant feature of E K Chambers' analysis of the play (1891) is the focus he puts on questions that were to provoke fierce debate throughout the next century. He links the play once again very clearly to contemporary Elizabethan politics and the debate over absolute monarchy. Shakespeare's history plays are the result of 'reflections on grave questions concerning the well-being of a nation'. In Chambers' view, Shakespeare finds 'the true foundation of regal authority' not in divine right, nor the will of parliament, but in 'the genuine king and leader of men . . . who best understands and sympathises with the needs and aspirations of his people, and is best fitted to guide them in the working out of their proper destiny'. By this token, both Richard II and Henry IV failed, while Henry V had 'all the notes of a true king'. Chambers also sees *King Richard II* and its sequel plays as a 'warning to a regardless nation' of 'the evils inherent in the Tudor conception of monarchy'. King Richard's deposition, he argues, looks forward 'with vague poetic foresight, to the scaffold outside Whitehall'.

The most influential mid twentieth-century critic of the play was E M W Tillyard, regarded as the founder of historical criticism, a school of thought which sees literature as reflecting the beliefs and assumptions of particular historical periods. His pioneering work, *Shakespeare's History Plays* (1944), which has since become the standard traditional interpretation of *King Richard II*, argues that the play endorses political stability: 'In doctrine the play is entirely orthodox.' Monarchs rule by divine right, rebellion is sinful and the Wars of the Roses are God's punishment for the deposition of King Richard II. Tillyard sees the 'formal and ceremonial' qualities of the play as creating a medieval world with Richard 'the last king of the old medieval order', which is then overtaken by the new and illegal modern world of Bullingbrook.

Modern critics have since challenged Tillyard's deeply conservative reading of the play. They accept that such views were powerful in Shakespeare's time, but argue that Elizabethan society was much more unstable, struggling to contain new radical ideas on political order and proper government. Tillyard dismisses, for example, the relevance of new humanist thinkers on politics and history such as Erasmus and Machiavelli, whose ideas are clearly present in the play (see Contexts section, pages 71–3). His critics argue that if Elizabethan society was as stable as Tillyard believed, how was it that civil war broke out just 40 years later over the very question posed in *King*

*Richard II*: How should England be governed? Nevertheless, Tillyard's book remains the most influential work on the history plays; setting much of the critical agenda for future critics.

John Dover Wilson, in his *Introduction to King Richard II* (1939), also focuses on the play's significance for Shakespeare's contemporaries, but presents a more complex view of the play than Tillyard, regarding it as both a personal and a political tragedy. Richard, for example, 'is to be viewed on a double plane of vision: at once realistically as a man, and symbolically as the royal martyr whose blood, spilt by the usurper, cries out for the vengeance which tears England asunder for two generations'. Dover Wilson also sees the play as driven and controlled by the concept of Fortune's wheel. Richard starts high up on the wheel 'exhibiting all the hubris and tyranny expected of persons in that position', while Bullingbrook in his banishment is down at the lowest point of his fortune.

Dover Wilson argues that, although the fortunes of the two kings may change, the play remains constantly in balance, taking sides neither with Richard nor with Bullingbrook. Shakespeare presents 'without concealment the weakness of the king's character, but he spares no pains to evoke our wholehearted pity for him in his fall'. Likewise, Bullingbrook is an opportunist, 'the puppet of Fortune', rather than a cunning schemer.

Lily B Campbell (1947) was particularly concerned with the significance *King Richard II* might have had for Shakespeare's contemporaries. 'To the sixteenth century, above all else a king was an administrator of justice, acting as God's deputy. And it is as God's justicer that Richard first appears. Shakespeare has given us the measuring rod of Richard's own conception of his office to judge by how far short he fails of his ideals'. Campbell also argues that many Elizabethans saw close parallels between King Richard and Queen Elizabeth I, accusing her of being swayed by favourites, leasing out her kingdom to favourites like Leicester and Essex, who 'became rich through her grants of land and special privileges, the farm of sweet wines to Essex, for instance'. She too was censured for spilling royal blood:

> In the minds of many Elizabethans, the blood of Mary Stuart cried from the ground against Elizabeth as did that of Thomas of Woodstock against Richard II.

Other critics, meanwhile, were focusing on the play's complexities of language, especially its imagery. Caroline Spurgeon in *Shakespeare's Imagery and What It Tells Us* (1935) identifies patterns of imagery in each of Shakespeare's plays and finds that the most continuous image in *King Richard II* is of 'the fruit and flower garden', noting the 'repeated use of the verbs "plant, pluck, crop, wither"'. She also remarks on other recurring images which she argues increase audience sympathy for Richard. He is portrayed as a careless gardener, a stricken tree, a fair rose, the rising sun, and the loss of his glory is 'like a shooting star' falling 'to the base earth from the firmament'.

Richard D Altick (1947) examines what he terms the play's iterative (repeated) images such as earth, blood, tears, disease and hollowness. He uses as his governing concept Pater's remark that the play's language has the unity and harmony of a musical composition to trace how such words and images appear and disappear, mingle and coalesce. M M Mahood in *Shakespeare's Wordplay* (1957) looks at what the play's imagery has to say about words and the power of language. (You can find these ideas illustrated in the Language section, pages 78–83.)

Later critics continued to differ in their interpretation of Richard's character. Pater's view of Richard as an artist-poet with the potential dignity of a tragic hero remained popular with a number of critics in the 1950s and 60s. Others saw him as a martyr-king like Charles I, as a clever, devious politician, or as a player-king, an actor unsuited to his role. Ernst Kantorowicz's *The King's Two Bodies* (1957) is one of the more significant readings of *King Richard II* of this period. Kantorowicz sees the play as an exploration of the 'godhead and manhood of a king'. In Tudor times political theory held that the king had two bodies: one physical and subject to human frailty, the other spiritual and incapable of human error (see page 72). Richard as king is a twin-like being and his tragedy is the inevitable failure of the man to carry out the superhuman responsibilities required of his office. 'The mirror scene is the climax of that tragedy of dual personality . . . The splintering mirror means, or is, the breaking apart of any possible duality.' John Barton's 1973 Royal Shakespeare Company production was particularly influenced by Kantorowicz's ideas (see page 101).

# Modern criticism

Modern criticism radically challenges the style and assumptions of earlier Shakespearian criticism, arguing that traditional interpretations, with their focus on character, are individualistic and misleading. The assumption that underlies most traditional criticism is that a play's meanings – or themes – are somehow 'in' the text and that these hidden meanings can be discovered through a close study of the text itself. More recent criticism, while acknowledging the importance of close reading, sees meaning in a text as being 'constructed' not 'found'. It is what the reader brings to the text, and the particular social, political and economic pressures on the text when it was written, that creates meaning. Such critics argue that the traditional critic's concentration on personal feelings results in a spurious objectivity which ignores society and history, and so divorces literary, dramatic and aesthetic matters from their social context. Further, their detachment from the real world makes them elitist, sexist and unpolitical.

Modern criticism of *King Richard II* has frequently returned to issues first raised by Tillyard about the way drama reflects the social conditions of its time and provoked distinct shifts in how the play is interpreted. The following discussion is organised under headings which represent major contemporary critical perspectives (political, feminist, performance, psychoanalytic, postmodern). But it is vital to appreciate that there is often overlap between the categories, and that to pigeonhole any example of criticism too precisely is to reduce its value and application.

## Political criticism

Political criticism is a convenient label for approaches concerned with power and social structure: in the world of the play, in Shakespeare's time and in our own. An early political critic is Jan Kott, who, in stark contrast to Kantorowicz's 'twin bodies' concept (see page 93), attempted to show how the play could be read as part of the modern world. Kott was a Polish scholar who fought with the Polish army and underground movement against the Nazis in the Second World War (1939–45), and had direct experience of the suffering and terror caused by Stalinist repression in Poland in the years that followed. His book *Shakespeare Our Contemporary* (1965) sees many parallels between the violence and cruelty of the modern world and the worlds of tyranny and despair that Shakespeare depicted.

For Kott, history is an oppressive force, and 'in Shakespeare, history itself is the drama'. What Kott has in mind here is the notion he develops in his discussion of Shakespeare's history plays: that history is a 'Grand Mechanism', a great staircase up which characters tread to their doom, each step 'marked by murder, perfidy, treachery' as ruler succeeds ruler. It does not matter if a character is good or bad, history will overwhelm them. Characters have little or no power over their lives, but are swept aside by inevitable social and historical forces beyond their control.

Kott argues that the working of the 'Grand Mechanism' is revealed all 'too brutally' in the abdication scene in *King Richard II*: it is 'the very moment when power was changing hands'. Kott especially draws attention to the play's final scene, which he judges terrifyingly matter-of-fact: 'A new reign has begun: six heads are being sent to the capital for the new king'.

Robert Ornstein (1972) challenges Tillyard's simplistic assumption that Elizabethans believed the historical Richard II was a rightful king sinfully deposed, claiming that most sixteenth-century writers in fact cite him as an example of 'royal lawlessness and incompetence' rather than 'martyred king'. Queen Elizabeth's remark about the play and the Earl of Essex's use of it as propaganda for his failed rebellion are given as further evidence that some Elizabethans at least saw things differently. Far from having a simple message, Ornstein sees an irony and paradox in Shakespeare's history plays. Plays like *King Richard II*, he argues, provide an illuminating perspective on how politics is the art of accommodation and survival, a skill which allows characters such as Bullingbrook and York to change allegiances, yet remain men of conscience.

Graham Holderness (1989) presents an interpretation which is almost the reverse of Tillyard's reading. For Holderness, it is not Richard who is the representative of feudalism but Bullingbrook. Far from endorsing order, the play shows the inherently unstable balance of power between a medieval feudal king and his nobles. Only with a strong and effective king could there be peace in the realm, but the stronger the king became the more uneasy and hostile were his nobles, since they regarded it as their natural right to share in the government of the country. The opening confrontation between Bullingbrook and King Richard (through Mowbray) is therefore just the latest episode in this feudal power struggle (see pages 4–5).

Furthermore, it is Richard not Bullingbrook who seeks to dismantle the feudal world of chivalric loyalty and replace it with absolute monarchical rule without reference to law or parliament.

In a later study (2000), Holderness is not so much concerned with contextualising the historical image of *King Richard II* within a grand historical narrative as with structuring his interpretation around antitheses such as 'past and present, absence and presence, male and female' and 'polarities such as nothing and something, language and silence, substance and shadow, image and reflection, womb and tomb'. He sees the play as depicting a history sharply differentiated from Shakespeare's own age. It peers 'through the medium of time into the past, seeing its contents with as much clarity and accuracy as contemporary knowledge could afford' but at the same time bears the imprint of contemporary Elizabethan life. So 'a male-dominated aristocracy preoccupied with war and military violence' is seen through the eyes of a society where the aristocracy was being 'marginalised and emasculated' by a female-led governing power. The play, Holderness argues, views a lost age of aristocratic glory 'with a complex consciousness of genuine regret and relieved resignation', lamenting the passing of 'antique chivalric prowess' while simultaneously casting a critical 'modern, civil and plebeian' eye at 'antiquity's destructive self-contradictions, its legacy of glamour and glory, absurdity and arrogance'.

Catherine Belsey, in her essay 'Making Histories', focuses on the relationship between language and power. Briefly, at the beginning of *King Richard II*, there seems a 'simple unity of names and things', which becomes progressively more tenuous. A word from the king can summon Mowbray and Bullingbrook to trial, initiate the Trial by Combat and then cancel it. The 'breath of kings' can banish one man for life, the other for ten years, then immediately reduce ten years to six, as if Richard's 'breath' had power over time itself.

The king's words, however, have authority only while they are part of 'the symbolic order' (i.e. the feudal chivalric code that binds king and nobles in mutual obligation). When the king attempts to make 'kingship' mean 'absolute monarchy' and illegally seizes Bullingbrook's inheritance, he breaks that 'symbolic code' creating 'a gap between names and things, between kingship and its referent, majesty'. Richard's words become increasingly empty of meaning and his destruction of the link between word and referent ensures that

'Bullingbrook's regime becomes in consequence one of bitter uncertainties, of conflicts of meaning which are simultaneously conflicts for power'. In this new world 'who is the traitor? Who is the king?'

## Feminist criticism

Feminism aims to achieve rights and equality for women in social, political and economic life. It challenges sexism: those beliefs and practices which result in the degradation, oppression and subordination of women. Feminist critics therefore reject 'male ownership' of criticism in which men determined what questions were to be asked of a play, and which answers were acceptable. They argue that male criticism often distorts women's points of view. It has become conventional to separate 'feminist' from political criticism, but in practice both forms of criticism are understandably interlinked, most typically by the notion of patriarchy (male domination of women) and misogyny (male hatred of women).

Linda Bamber and Coppelia Kahn offer interestingly different descriptions of the relationship between femininity, masculinity and history in *King Richard II*. Bamber sees 'femininity' and 'history' as two diametrically opposed and mutually incompatible contraries, the feminine world of the play being a kind of emblem of what the masculine world wishes to exclude: 'The world of men offers political and military adventure and a headlong struggle for power'. Isabel is 'queen of an alternative realm, the realm of the garden', a private world 'slow, full of a sorrow that cannot be released in action'. Neither Isabel nor the Duchess of Gloucester can influence the male political world and even when the Duchess of York successfully challenges masculine values her efforts seem misogynistically offered only as 'a comic contrast to the seriousness of the world of men'.

Kahn (1981) believes Shakespeare makes the late medieval world of King Richard II 'a mirror of his own by stressing its obsession with paternal authority and power'. First Gaunt, then York remind Richard of his paternal heritage and the need to live up to the ideals of his father and grandfather. But Richard does not seem to hear them. On his return from Ireland he speaks to his kingdom as if it were the source of maternal comfort: 'As the good mother, she comforts Richard with flowers and sweets' and 'repulses his enemies with spiders, toads, nettles and adders'. Bullingbrook, on the other hand identifies with his father from the start. He is unwilling to 'seem crestfallen' in his 'father's sight', salutes his father as 'the earthly author' of his blood and returns from exile professing to claim only his paternal rights. Where Bullingbrook is single-minded, Richard swings 'between fullness and emptiness, omnipotence or total dejection, because he is emotionally dependent on a boundless supply of reassurance, maternal in origin and quality, which the real world cannot supply'.

Jean Howard and Phyllis Rackin (1997) take up the concept put forward by many critics that the struggle between Richard and Bullingbrook is a conflict between two styles of royal authority. Richard is the hereditary medieval monarch whose authority is expressed in ceremonial ritual; Bullingbrook achieves his authority through personal performance and 'the politically motivated theatrical self-presentation of a modern ruler'. Howard and Rackin note how Queen Elizabeth I deliberately claimed masculine authority by referring to herself as a 'prince' and they argue that the play's 'binary opposition' also invited Elizabethan audiences to ponder their own conceptions of 'masculinity' and 'femininity':

> In *Richard II*, the king's patrilineal authority is vitiated by his
> womanish tears and his effeminate behaviour: he has no taste
> for foreign wars, he talks when he should act, and he wastes
> his kingdom's treasure by indulging in excessive luxuries.
> Bullingbrook, who has no hereditary right to the crown,
> acquires it by the successful performance of masculine virtues.

Margaret Healey (1998) believes that the play 'subjects male roles to radical scrutiny' primarily by highlighting the considerable difference between what the men say and what they do. In the opening scene, for example, Mowbray vows to refrain from indulging in 'a woman's war' of words with Bullingbrook, but all the audience gets to see is 'the two men doing precisely this – warring with words at great length whilst "dolled up to the nines" in chivalric tournament gear'. Surely, Healey argues, 'such boastful pretensions to virility and manhood as Mowbray's and the feudal peers' in the gage scene – effectively another "bitter war" of "eager tongues" between men – are being consciously undermined by such theatrical manipulations?'

Healey also notes how at times in the play, gender roles seem to be reversed. The Duchess of Gloucester angrily questions Gaunt's manhood before branding him a coward. In the streets of London, Queen Isabel takes her dejected husband to task and urges him on to more manly resistance. The Duchess of York saves her son's life with a 'masculine' single-mindedness and determination, while Bullingbrook, in contrast, is depicted in the final scene 'as a concerned father who appears to take his nurturing responsibilities seriously'. Ironically, if only the 'womanish' Richard had possessed 'the more positive "feminine" qualities – namely the ability to see obliquely, and to nurture – both Richard and his realm would have fared better'.

## Performance criticism

Performance criticism fully acknowledges that *King Richard II* is a play: a script to be performed by actors to an audience. It examines all aspects of the play in performance: its staging in the theatre or on film and video. Performance criticism focuses on Shakespeare's stagecraft and the semiotics of theatre (signs: words, costumes, gestures, etc.), together with the 'afterlife' of the play (what happened to *King Richard II* after Shakespeare wrote it). That involves scrutiny of how productions at different periods have presented the play. As such, performance criticism appraises how the text has been cut, added to, rewritten and rearranged to present a version felt appropriate to the times.

The potentially subversive nature of *King Richard II* when it was first performed in the late 1590s and its dangerous involvement in the Earl of Essex's abortive rebellion has already been outlined in the Contexts section (pages 69–70). Apart from the mention of a performance at the Globe Theatre, on June 12th, 1631 'before a good audience', there is little documentary evidence of how frequently the play was performed in the early part of the seventeenth century before civil war broke out in 1642 and the theatres were closed. When they were opened again following the restoration of the monarchy, Nahum Tate staged his adaptation of the play (see pages 89–90). Although he set it in Sicily, renamed it *The Sicilian Usurper*, omitted mention of almost all of Richard's crimes and painted the usurper Bullingbrook in a villainous light, it was still not enough to prevent the play from being banned by Charles II, mindful no doubt of the deposition and execution of his own father, Charles I.

The play lost favour in the eighteenth century and was rarely performed, but Lewis Theobald's adaptation in 1719 met with considerable success. As with Tate's adaptation, the changes Theobald made to the play reflect the taste of early eighteenth-century bourgeois audiences for admirable heroes and sentimental romance. For example, he pushes the play even further into sentimentality than Tate, not least by having Aumerle fall desperately in love with Northumberland's newly created daughter, the Lady Piercy. Then, when Aumerle is executed for his loyalty to Richard, he has Lady Piercy take her own life.

The play was more popular in the nineteenth century and the personality of Richard the tragic hero now dominated the stage. Productions also sought to create spectacle and sensation, paying detailed attention to the creation of sets and costumes appropriate to late fourteenth-century England. In 1857, Charles Kean staged a particularly spectacular production, with amazingly lifelike dummy horses for the combat scene and an additional 'show-stopping' scene presenting Bullingbrook's triumphant entry into London, which used nearly 600 extras and filled the stage with movement, colour and incident.

Frank Benson's highly praised 1896 production still retained some of the visually spectacular qualities of earlier nineteenth-century productions, but offered also an imaginative response to the play's language and characterisation. In the opening scene, for example, Benson, as Richard, casually fed and stroked his hounds while Bullingbrook and Mowbray accused each other. Then, at the end of the combat scene, Richard's favourite wolfhound (just as Froissart recorded in his chronicle) left Richard to follow Bullingbrook.

The early twentieth century saw a return to much simpler stagings of the play. Most productions no longer attempted to create an impression of realism. Under the influence of William Poel and Harley Granville Barker, the stage was cleared of the clutter of historical detail and elaborate sets. The aim was to recapture the conditions of the Elizabethan bare stage, which was not concerned with theatrical illusion. That implied simple impressionistic sets, continuous action, lightly cut scripts and a concern for clear, more natural speaking of Shakespeare's language.

The effect of these changes is very evident in Harcourt Williams' 1929 production. Because little time was needed for elaborate set changes, far more of Shakespeare's script could be included. The actors abandoned what Williams called 'the slow deliberate method of delivering Shakespeare's verse, and the absurd convention of the Shakespearean voice', speaking instead with a swift natural inflection. The undoubted master of this new style of verse-speaking was John Gielgud, who played Richard. Reviewers commented on how Gielgud spoke the 'glorious verse clearly and rhythmically', his voice drawing out 'the musicality and elegaic tones, the petulance and pathos of the sad king'.

In 1968, Ian McKellen played a radically different Richard to the effeminately glittering interpretations that had gone before. His Richard was caught up in the power of ceremonial duty, insulated from reality since childhood by total obedience to his slightest wish. McKellen's interpretation was rooted in the idea of family. He believed Shakespeare's script repeatedly emphasises kinship and blood-ties: 'Everyone at its centre is related by the blood which will be spilled during the ensuing civil wars.' Shallow and heartless at first, the turning point for McKellen's Richard came at the 'need friends' speech, which came out as a great cry of anguish.

John Barton's highly stylised 1973 Royal Shakespeare Company production was a most ambitious and influential interpretation which emphasised the balanced doubleness of the play by casting two actors to play the parts of Richard and Bullingbrook on successive nights. Richard Pasco played a sensitive and poetic Richard one night and Ian Richardson played a cunning, dangerously unpredictable Richard the next. A variety of symbols and special effects were also introduced to convey the play's balanced structure and highlight the theatricality of kingship. There were actual buckets on stage to illustrate Richard's 'buckets and well' speech. A dish of soil at the front of the stage provided Gaunt with some English earth to take up during his patriotic 'sceptred isle' speech and a snowman gave visual expression to the 'mockery king of snow' lines.

Although Barton's production was criticised for its 'gimmicks', many felt it to be innovative and powerful and its success encouraged subsequent productions to move away from the old traditional interpretations. The 1988 Phoenix Theatre production, for example, showed a harsh, dark, metallic England. In the early scenes, Derek Jacobi played Richard as a callous, even brutish, tyrant who believed he was rendered all-powerful by the mystic power of kingship, and who shocked even his own courtiers by the blow he aimed at the dying Gaunt. Yet amazingly, this tyrant took on dignity and grace as he rid himself of the trappings of office.

The most innovative production of the late twentieth century was Deborah Warner's 1995 production at the Royal National Theatre, with Fiona Shaw as the king. Shaw played the role with intense nervous energy, rapid changes of mood and awkward assertions of authority. She would sit mischievously on the throne, her legs dangling off the floor, constantly fidgeting, sucking her thumb, playing piggyback with Aumerle and even carrying her crown around in a shopping basket. Richard's relationship with Bullingbrook seemed more like sister and brother as Shaw constantly looked to him for approval or to gauge his strength. Richard's queen was played as a wise and caring mother-cum-wife to Richard's neurotic, unreasonable boy-king.

The history of Shakespeare's *King Richard II* in performance clearly demonstrates its ability to move audiences of different cultures in varied and sometimes surprising ways. One of the most surprisingly moving performances that Ian McKellen remembers (quoted in *Playing Shakespeare* by John Barton, Methuen Press, 1984), was when he toured as Richard in a production that briefly visited Czechoslovakia six months after the Czech Prime Minister, Dubček, had been forcibly removed from office by invading Russian troops:

> When I came to the speech where Richard II returns from Ireland to discover that his nation has been overrun by his cousin Bullingbrook, and he kneels down on the earth and asks the stones and the nettles and the insects to help him in his helpless state against the armies who had invaded his land, I could hear something I had never heard before, nor since, which was the whole audience apparently weeping. It shakes me now to think about it, because in that instant I realised that the audience were crying for themselves. They recognised in Richard II their own predicament of only six months previously when their neighbours and as it were their cousins had invaded their land, and all they had were sticks and stones to throw at the tanks.
>
> I would never have talked about the play in those terms. We hadn't seen it as directly relevant to any modern political

situation. Shakespeare could not have known about communism, about the East or the West. Afterwards I said to one of the new men, the anti-Dubček faction, to one of their leaders who was in the audience, 'Who did you side with in the play, Richard II or Bullingbrook? The man on the ground or the invader?' And he said, 'Both right, both wrong.'

## Psychoanalytic criticism

In the twentieth century, psychoanalysis became a major influence on the understanding and interpretation of human behaviour. The founder of psychoanalysis, Sigmund Freud, explained personality as the result of unconscious and irrational desires, repressed memories or wishes, sexuality, fantasy, anxiety and conflict. Freud's theories have had a strong influence on criticism and stagings of Shakespeare's plays, most famously on *Hamlet* in the well-known claim that Hamlet suffers from an Oedipus complex.

*King Richard II*, even though possessing a central character so evidently caught up with his own narcissistic emotions, has attracted comparatively little attention from critics who adopt a psychoanalytic approach to Shakespeare's plays. There seems to be no genuinely sustained psychoanalytic interpretation of the play, only allusions to specific features. For example, one critic asserted that Richard suffered from a 'diseased mentality' and a 'God-complex'. Charles Forker (1998) provides a brief but helpful summary of other fragmentary psychoanalytic interpretations:

- Richard and Bullingbrook represent contrasting images of kingship. Richard's is 'maternal' and nurturing, Bullingbrook's is 'paternal' and power-oriented.
- In the course of the play, Richard undergoes a 'psychological transformation' from sentimentality to mature awareness of others.
- Richard is a psychotic, with a strong death wish, but a weak libido (sexual drive).
- The play explores the presentation of family (in particular father–son) relationships in the play. Richard bears the burden of having had a famous father and there are hints of an 'oedipal relationship' between York and Aumerle (another interpretation sees this father–son relationship characterised by an element of guilt).

- Questions of identity and perception in the play are related to 'experiences of loss, absence, negativity and nothingness' as Shakespeare attempts to dramatise psychological inwardness (for example, Richard's shattering of the mirror gives Richard's feelings theatrical presence and substance).

Such interpretations demonstrate the weaknesses in applying psychoanalytic theories to *King Richard II*. They cannot be proved or disproved, and they are highly speculative. Psychoanalytic approaches are therefore often accused of imposing interpretations based on theory rather than on Shakespeare's text. However, Richard's evidently troubled sense of self has attracted some critics to the possibility of psychoanalytic interpretations of the play.

## Postmodern criticism

Postmodern criticism (sometimes called 'deconstruction' or 'poststructuralism') is often difficult to understand because it is not centrally concerned with consistency or reasoned argument. It does not accept that one section of the story is necessarily connected to what follows, or that characters relate to each other in meaningful ways. The approach therefore has obvious drawbacks in providing a model for examination students who are expected to display reasoned, coherent argument, and respect for the evidence of the text.

Postmodern approaches are most clearly seen in stage productions which self-consciously show little regard for consistency in character, or for coherence in telling the story. There, you could think of it as simply 'a mixture of styles', with actors dressed in costumes from very different historical periods. *King Richard II* is almost always presented in a style that suggests medieval England, but occasionally 'disruptive' elements are added. For example, in the Royal Shakespeare Company's outstanding 2000 production, Harry Hotspur (Percy) first appeared like a modern SAS soldier with beret and gun belt.

Some postmodern critics focus on minor or marginal characters, or on gaps or silences in the play. They claim that these features, previously overlooked as unimportant, reveal significant truths about the play. But postmodern criticism most typically revels in the cleverness of its own use of language, and accepts all kinds of anomalies and contradictions in a spirit of playfulness or 'carnival'. It abandons any notion of the organic unity of the play, and rejects the assumption that a Shakespeare play possesses clear patterns or themes.

*King Richard II* (like other history plays) has attracted little sustained postmodern criticism. That is probably because the play's historical context, its clear storyline, and the evident concern with politics and character, resists such 'playful' approaches. When postmodern critics do occasionally address the play, they tend to focus on Richard's language: excessive, hyperbolic, self-indulgent and often expressing what he desires or fantasises, rather than what is real (for example, claiming great strength when in fact he is powerless). Terry Eagleton (1986) uses the vocabulary of the postmodern critic, but his comments on the play amount to little more than that Richard frequently deludes himself. For example, he comments on how 'Shakespeare is continually struck by the "nothing" of language which is detached from the real world, its lack of ground or substance, and which yet has power to bend the world to its own will'. But language, as Richard discovers, is not all-powerful – 'it hovers between nullity and omnipotence. There is a recalcitrance about the material world that language cannot dissolve.' Eagleton's conclusion: 'How real is the signifier is a question which *King Richard II* constantly poses' means little more than traditional criticism's recognition that Richard is given to fantasising ('signifier' = word).

# Organising your responses

The purpose of this section is to help you improve your writing about *King Richard II*. It offers practical guidance on two kinds of tasks: writing about an extract from the play and writing an essay. Whether you are answering an examination question, preparing coursework (term papers), or carrying out research into your own chosen topic, this section will help you organise and present your responses.

In all your writing, there are three vital things to remember:

- *King Richard II* is a play. Although it is usually referred to as a 'text', *King Richard II* is not a book, but a script intended to be acted on a stage. So your writing should demonstrate an awareness of the play in performance as theatre. That means you should always try to read the play with an 'inner eye', thinking about how it could look and sound on stage. By doing so, you will be able to write effectively about Shakespeare's language and dramatic techniques.

- *King Richard II* is not a presentation of 'reality'. It is a dramatic construct in which the playwright, through theatre, engages the emotions and intellect of the audience. The characters and story may persuade an audience to suspend its disbelief for several hours. The audience may identify with the characters, be deeply moved by them, and may think of them as if they were living human beings. However, when you write, a major part of your task is to show how Shakespeare achieves his dramatic effects that so engage the audience.

- How Shakespeare learned his craft. As a schoolboy, and in his early years as a dramatist, Shakespeare used all kinds of models or frameworks to guide his writing. But he quickly learned how to vary and adapt the models to his own dramatic purposes. This section offers frameworks that you can use to structure your writing. As you use them, follow Shakespeare's example! Adapt them to suit your own writing style and needs.

## Writing about an extract

It is an expected part of all Shakespeare study that you should be able to write well about an extract (sometimes called a 'passage') from the play. An extract is usually between 30 and 70 lines long, and you are invited to comment on it. The instructions vary. Sometimes the task is very briefly expressed:

- Write a detailed commentary on the following passage.
  or
- Write about the effect of the extract on your own thoughts and feelings.

At other times a particular focus is specified for your writing:

- With close reference to the language and imagery of the passage, show in what ways it helps to establish important issues in the play.
  or
- Analyse the style and structure of the extract, showing what it contributes to your appreciation of the play's major concerns.

In writing your response, you must of course take account of the precise wording of the task, and ensure you concentrate on each particular point specified. But however the invitation to write about an extract is expressed, it requires you to comment in detail on the language. You should identify and evaluate how the language reveals character, contributes to plot development, offers opportunities for dramatic effect, and embodies crucial concerns of the play as a whole. These 'crucial concerns' are also referred to as the 'themes', or 'issues', or 'preoccupations' of the play.

The following framework is a guide to how you can write a detailed commentary on an extract. Writing a paragraph or more on each item will help you bring out the meaning and significance of the extract, and show how Shakespeare achieves his effects.

---

**Paragraph 1:** Locate the extract in the play and identify who is on stage.

**Paragraph 2:** State what the extract is about and identify its structure.

**Paragraph 3:** Identify the mood or atmosphere of the extract.

---

| **Paragraphs 4–8:** | These paragraphs analyse how |
| Diction (vocabulary) | Shakespeare achieves his effects. They |
| Imagery | concentrate on the language of the |
| Antithesis | extract, showing the dramatic effect of |
| Repetition | each item, and how the language |
| Lists | expresses crucial concerns of the play. |

**Paragraph 9:** Staging opportunities

**Paragraph 10:** Conclusion

The analysis and examples of different types of language used in this Guide (imagery, antithesis, etc., see pages 76–88) will help you in constructing your own response. And because *King Richard II* is written entirely in verse appropriate to its varying moods and situations, you should also remember to comment on the style of the verse in any particular extract. The following example uses the framework to show how the paragraphs making up the essay might be written. The framework headings (in bold), would not of course appear in your essay. They are presented only to help you see how the framework is used. The extract is from Act 4 Scene 1, lines 162–220. (You may also find it helpful to read how the passage is discussed in the Commentary, pages 43–5.)

## Extract

RICHARD  Alack, why am I sent for to a king
     Before I have shook off the regal thoughts
     Wherewith I reigned? I hardly yet have learned
     To insinuate, flatter, bow and bend my knee.
     Give sorrow leave awhile to tutor me           5
     To this submission. Yet I well remember
     The favours of these men. Were they not mine?
     Did they not sometime cry 'All hail' to me?
     So Judas did to Christ, but he in twelve
     Found truth in all but one, I in twelve thousand none.    10
     God save the king! Will no man say Amen?
     Am I both priest and clerk? Well then, Amen.
     God save the king, although I be not he,
     And yet Amen if heaven do think him me.
     To do what service am I sent for hither?          15

YORK  To do that office of thine own good will
        Which tirèd majesty did make thee offer,
        The resignation of thy state and crown
        To Henry Bullingbrook.
RICHARD  Give me the crown. Here, cousin, seize the crown,          20
        On this side my hand and on that side thine.
        Now is this golden crown like a deep well
        That owes two buckets, filling one another,
        The emptier ever dancing in the air,
        The other down, unseen and full of water.                   25
        That bucket, down and full of tears, am I,
        Drinking my griefs whilst you mount up on high.
BULLINGBROOK  I thought you had been willing to resign.
RICHARD  My crown I am, but still my griefs are mine.
        You may my glories and my state depose,                     30
        But not my griefs. Still am I king of those.
BULLINGBROOK  Part of your cares you give me with your crown.
RICHARD  Your cares set up do not pluck my cares down.
        My care is loss of care, by old care done.
        Your care is gain of care, by new care won.                 35
        The cares I give I have, though given away.
        They 'tend the crown, yet still with me they stay.
BULLINGBROOK  Are you contented to resign the crown?
RICHARD  Aye – no. No – aye, for I must nothing be,
        Therefore no 'no', for I resign to thee.                    40
        Now, mark me how I will undo myself.
        I give this heavy weight from off my head
        And this unwieldy sceptre from my hand,
        The pride of kingly sway from out my heart.
        With mine own tears I wash away my balm;                    45
        With mine own hands I give away my crown;
        With mine own tongue deny my sacred state;
        With mine own breath release all duteous oaths.
        All pomp and majesty I do forswear;
        My manors, rents, revenues I forgo;                         50
        My acts, decrees, and statutes I deny.
        God pardon all oaths that are broke to me;
        God keep all vows unbroke are made to thee.
        Make me that nothing have with nothing grieved,

And thou with all pleased that hast all achieved.                    55
Long mayst thou live in Richard's seat to sit,
And soon lie Richard in an earthy pit.
God save King Henry, unkinged Richard says,
And send him many years of sunshine days.

**Paragraph 1: Locate the extract in the play and identify who is on stage.**
Richard has been taken prisoner by Henry Bullingbrook. Henry has
called a special session of Parliament in order to convince the House
of Lords that Richard has voluntarily abdicated the throne and named
himself as legitimate successor. But he has just been fiercely
denounced as a traitor by the Bishop of Carlisle, who prophesies such
an unlawful act will result in bloody ruin for England.

**Paragraph 2: State what the extract is about and identify its structure.**
(Begin with one or two sentences identifying what the extract is about,
followed by several sentences briefly identifying its structure, that is,
the unfolding events and the different sections of the extract.)
    The extract is the beginning of the episode which dramatises the
central historical event of the play: the deposition of the rightful King
Richard by the usurper Henry Bullingbrook. In tones of bitter irony,
Richard expresses dismay that his former followers have abandoned
him so quickly, then increasingly taunts Bullingbrook, keeping him
waiting for his agreement. But in the extract's final speech, in verse of
great formality, Richard strips himself of the symbols and rights of
England's kingship, wishes for death, and acclaims 'King Henry'.

**Paragraph 3: Identify the mood or atmosphere of the extract.**
The dominant mood is intensely ceremonial, as should befit the event:
the resignation of one king and the crowning of another. But
Shakespeare varies the atmosphere from speech to speech, as the
defeated king uses all his rhetorical power to dominate the stage.
Richard begins ironically, deriding the speed with which his
deposition has been arranged, giving him no time to learn the
humiliations of submission. He then causes the assembled nobles to
feel shame or embarrassment at their total betrayal of him, as Judas
betrayed Jesus. Next, Richard causes Bullingbrook to feel increasing
exasperation as, using imagery and wordplay, he delays his
resignation. But at last Richard consents, and the mood becomes

ritualistic and stately. In measured verse, like that of a religious liturgy, he divests himself of all the signs and powers of a king. But there are hints of disdain, changing to despair in lines 56–7, and the final two lines can create a feeling of ironic mockery.

### Paragraph 4: Diction (vocabulary)

For all the ceremony of the occasion, and the detailed references to the symbols of kingship, certain very 'ordinary' words add dramatic depth. Richard's use of 'favours' (line 7) carries meanings that intensify his condemnation of his former followers and their feelings of shame, for the word can refer to the good services they gave him as king, the gifts or tokens they gave him, the loyalty they expressed through their costumes, or even to their faces. Similarly, when Richard asks everyone to mark how he will 'undo' himself, the simple word is charged with different meanings: humiliate himself, give away the tokens of kingship, or destroy his identity. But his remarkable 'Aye – no. No – aye' (line 39) especially catches Richard's deeply equivocal feeling at being forced to hand over power to Bullingbrook. The expression, and the 'no "no"' that follows can sustain multiple interpretations, not least because, when spoken on stage, 'Aye' can sound like 'I', and 'no' like 'know'.

### Paragraph 5: Imagery

The vivid imagery in the passage echoes many of the images and themes that run through the play. They also display Richard's capacity for self-dramatisation and hyperbole, as, for example, in his comparison of himself to Christ betrayed by Judas. Richard typically exaggerates, claiming that whilst only one in twelve of Jesus' disciples proved not to be faithful, twelve thousand of his own followers have deserted him. Richard then develops an extended image of the crown as a deep well within which two buckets hang. The image is yet another expression of the play's many 'balances' or 'weighings', particularly that of Richard and Bullingbrook.

In Richard's final speech, images are fused with action as he ritualistically hands over the symbols of his office. Yet again he cannot resist the imagery of his tears, which he claims now wash away the balm with which he was anointed (and which stands in striking contrast to an earlier claim he made that 'not all the water in the rough rude sea' could wash away that balm). Ironically, the extract ends with perhaps the play's most persistent image of kingship: the king as the sun. But this time it is for King Henry that Richard wishes 'many years of sunshine days'.

### Paragraph 6: Antithesis

The conflict between Richard and Henry that characterises the entire play finds subtle expression in the antitheses in the passage, not least in how 'I' and 'my' are insistently pitted against 'you' and 'your' throughout. The antithesis of the contrasting buckets has just been noted, in which 'down' is opposed to 'mount up on high', and is echoed in the 'up' and 'down' of cares in line 33. Elsewhere, Richard self-indulgently sets his former 'glories' against his 'griefs'. Then too, there are the stark contradictions of 'Aye – no. No – aye' which accurately express Richard's inner turmoil. As he formally renounces power, 'pardon all oaths' is set against 'keep all vows', and Richard looks forward to having 'nothing' whilst Bullingbrook has 'all'. But perhaps the most succinct and telling antithesis is in the penultimate line, which precisely reflects what has occurred: 'King Henry' and 'unkinged Richard'.

### Paragraph 7: Repetition

The repetition of certain words heightens dramatic effect. Richard's entire final speech is ritualistic (it has been described as an inverted rite of coronation), and repetition is central to ritual and ceremony. The repetitions of rhythm and words are strikingly obvious as, line by line, Richard renounces the trappings and authority of kingship. In his final eight lines he switches to rhyming couplets, which adds further repetitive force. But elsewhere in the passage, repetition achieves subtle effects, particularly in lines 33–6, where, in response to Bullingbrook's 'cares', Richard plays nine times upon the word, exploiting its wide range of meanings (responsibilities, efforts, sorrows, concerns, desire, anxieties).

### Paragraph 8: Lists

Shakespeare's technique of piling item on item ('copiousness') is evident in Richard's final self-deposition speech, as one by one he ceremonially divests himself of all his royal powers. Just as a coronation ceremony is a carefully staged sequence of distinct events, so Richard recapitulates that catalogue in reverse (he mentions over a dozen items, including such shorter catalogues as 'manors, rents, revenues', to imply the comprehensiveness of what he has lost). Elsewhere Shakespeare uses the same technique for different dramatic effect. There is an implied sneer in the list of things he has yet to learn as a subject, 'insinuate, flatter, bow and bend my knee' (perhaps accompanied by a scornful gaze at all his nobles who have already learned such obsequious actions).

### Paragraph 9: Staging opportunities

The extract offers opportunities for thrilling theatrical presentation. Although Richard is surrounded by his enemies (or men who no longer support him), he is without doubt the centre of dramatic focus. Bullingbrook holds all the political power, but Richard has full theatrical command of the stage, and he uses all his histrionic ability to ensure that although he is humiliated, he is in control of the drama. He is centre stage throughout, the focus of audience attention, and he stage-manages his deposition (particularly in his final speech) with great ceremony and dignity. With his former nobles ranged around him, and facing Bullingbrook, he determines the pace, mood and conduct of his overthrow. Initially imperious and accusatory he shames the nobility. Then by imagery and wordplay he reduces Bullingbrook to linguistic impotence and impatient one-line protests. Finally, in a speech that can be delivered in any number of ways, ranging from confident bravura to resigned defeat, he makes clear the full significance of transferring power and position, and ends with an ironic jibe at Bullingbrook. The extract demands a ceremonious staging, with Richard always in control.

### Paragraph 10: Conclusion

The extract displays the power of rhetoric, the way in which language can be used to persuade, to express, but also to overcome reality. Richard is weak, his political power gone. Bullingbrook is strong, the master of realpolitik. But it is Richard who dominates. The extract is the dramatic climax of the play, as the crown passes from one man to another. It reveals most vividly Richard's tendency to self-pity and self-dramatisation and, more movingly, the way he uses language to express powerfully and precisely the enormity of what is taking place, most obviously in the formality and solemn ritual phrasing of his 'dis-coronation' (or 'unkinging').

# Writing an essay

As part of your study of *King Richard II* you will be asked to write essays, either under examination conditions or for coursework (term papers). Examinations mean that you are under pressure of time, usually having around one hour to prepare and write each essay. Coursework means that you have much longer to think about and produce your essay. But whatever the type of essay, each will require you to develop an argument about a particular aspect of *King Richard II*.

The essays you write on *King Richard II* require you to set out your thoughts on a particular aspect of the play, using evidence from the text. The people who read your essays (examiners, teachers, lecturers) will have certain expectations of your writing. In each essay they will expect you to discuss and analyse a particular topic, using evidence from the play to develop an argument in an organised, coherent and persuasive way. Examiners look for, and reward, what they call 'an informed personal response'. This simply means that you show you have good knowledge of the play ('informed') and can use evidence from it to support and justify your own viewpoint ('personal').

You should write at different levels, moving beyond description to analysis and evaluation. Simply telling the story or describing characters is not as effective as analysing how events or characters embody wider concerns of the play: its themes, issues, preoccupations. In your writing, always give practical examples (quotations, actions) which illustrate the themes you discuss. The following threefold structure can help you organise your response:

opening paragraph
developing paragraphs
concluding paragraph.

*Opening paragraph* Begin with a paragraph identifying just what topic or issue you will focus on. Show that you have understood what the question is about. You probably will have prepared for particular topics. But look closely at the question and identify key words to see what particular aspect it asks you to write about. Adapt your material to answer that question. Examiners do not reward an essay, however well-written, if it is not on the question set.

*Developing paragraphs* This is the main body of your essay. In it, you develop your argument, point by point, paragraph by paragraph. Use evidence from the play that illuminates the topic or issue, and answers the question set. Each paragraph makes a point of dramatic or thematic significance. Some paragraphs could make points concerned with context or particular critical approaches. The effect of your argument builds up as each paragraph adds to the persuasive quality of your essay. Use brief quotations that support your argument, and show clearly just why they are relevant. Ensure that your essay demonstrates that you are aware that *King Richard II* is a play, a drama intended for performance, and therefore open to a wide variety of interpretations and audience response.

*Concluding paragraph* Your final paragraph pulls together your main conclusions. It does not simply repeat what you have written earlier, but summarises concisely how your essay has successfully answered the question.

## Example

Question: How far do you agree that England is the central character in *King Richard II*?

The following notes show the 'ingredients' of an answer. In an examination it is usually helpful to prepare similar notes from which you write your essay, paragraph by paragraph. To help you understand how contextual matters or points from different critical approaches might be included, the words 'Context' or 'Criticism' appear before some items. Remember that examiners are not impressed by 'name-dropping': use of critics' names. What they want you to show is your knowledge and judgement of the play and its contexts, and of how it has been interpreted from different critical perspectives.

**Opening paragraph**

Examiners will be looking for how well you can develop an argument, so include the following points and aim to write a sentence or more on each:

- Criticism Many critics have made such a claim, but phrase it in different ways: for example, the play is about 'the matter of England', presents a 'vision of England' or creates a 'tapestry of England'.
- Shakespeare indicates in the dialogue the precise English locality of many scenes: Coventry, Ravensburgh, Gloucestershire hills, Berkeley, Harlech, and Flint castles.
- But is England 'the central character'? Richard and Bullingbrook fit that description because the play's primary focus is on their fall and rise. England cannot strictly speaking be regarded as a character because it neither speaks nor takes any active part in events.
- Context Yet England does feature significantly in the play in that so many characters speak of it with concern, knowing all too well that their country's future is inextricably bound up with the fate of the king.
- This essay will therefore focus on how England becomes a constant presence in the play, a vision or ideal which shifts its perspective as it passes through the minds of different characters.

**Developing paragraphs**

- *England as an object of patriotic pride*: Bullingbrook leaves for exile determined to remain 'a true born Englishman' (Act 1 Scene 3, line 308). York disapproves of Richard's love of foreign fashions (Act 2 Scene 1, line 21). Exile condemns Mowbray to a 'speechless death' because he can no longer speak his native tongue (Act 1 Scene 3, lines 159–73).
- Context *England past and present*: In his deathbed speech (Act 2 Scene 1, lines 40–68), Gaunt presents two visions of England that other characters constantly echo. First he recalls with pride the England of his youth, a warrior's world, a 'fortress' guarded by a 'happy breed of men' renowned and feared throughout the world for 'Christian service and true chivalry'. This idealised world is then contemptuously contrasted with Richard's new modern England (lines 59–68), mortgaged out to businessmen and lawyers with their 'inky blots and rotten parchment bonds'.

- Context *Who owns England?*: Richard clearly regards it as his personal property to be exploited as he chooses (Act 1 Scene 4, lines 42–63). The passionate declarations of a special spiritual bond between a king and his country (Act 3 Scene 2, lines 4–62) come only when he realises he might lose his kingdom to Bullingbrook.

  The hostile nobles likewise believe they have a right to a share of England. They resent Richard's promotion of lesser nobles at their expense ('Base men by his endowments are made great' Act 2 Scene 3, line 138). Bullingbrook makes very clear to Bushy and Green what he believes are his personal rights of ownership in Act 3 Scene 1, lines 22–7.

- Context *England the helpless victim*: At Flint Castle (Act 3 Scene 3), both rivals conjure up images of the suffering England will endure if they do not get their way: Bullingbrook will 'bedrench / The fresh green lap of fair King Richard's land' with crimson blood if his inheritance is not restored (lines 42–8), while Richard foresees 'the flower of England's face' made scarlet with the 'bloody crowns of mothers' sons' if Bullingbrook refuses to submit (lines 91–100). The Bishop of Carlisle sees England as the land 'of dead men's skulls' if Richard is deposed (Act 4 Scene 1, lines 136–49).

- *England as a garden or farm*: In the allegorical scene at the heart of the play (Act 3 Scene 4) Shakespeare presents two symbolic visions of England: as an idyllic Garden of Eden where Richard and his queen live in luxurious ease (lines 1–20) and a real garden requiring constant hard work and attention, a duty of care that Richard has clearly failed to fulfil (lines 54–66). This vision of England as a garden or farm requiring hard work (ploughing, manuring, watering) is echoed many times elsewhere in the play, most ominously in the final scene where Bullingbrook regrets that Richard's blood should 'sprinkle' him to make him grow (Act 5 Scene 6, lines 45–6).

### Concluding paragraph

- The play both celebrates and reflects on the importance of England and how it should be governed: whether by divinely appointed absolute monarch, feudal alliance of king and nobles or monarch pledged to govern for the 'common-wealth'.
- Context How England should be governed is a key issue in Shakespeare's sequel plays. *King Richard II* is just one part of a

series of explorations of the burdens, skills and duties of kingship (see pages 62–3).

- Criticism The play conveys a deep sense of the fragility of English national unity and ends in an uneasy peace.
- England may not be a 'character', but it is certainly one of the play's major preoccupations.

## Writing about character

Much critical writing about *King Richard II* traditionally focused on characters, writing about them as if they were living human beings. Today it is not sufficient just to describe their personalities. When you write about characters you will also be expected to show that they are dramatic constructs, part of Shakespeare's stagecraft, instruments of his exploration of politics. They embody the wider concerns of the play, have certain dramatic functions, and are set in a social and political world with particular values and beliefs. They reflect and express issues of significance to Shakespeare's society – and today's.

Of course you should say what a character seems like to you, but you should also write about how Shakespeare makes him or her part of his overall dramatic design. But there is a danger in merely writing about the functions of characters or the character types they represent, for to reduce a character to a mere plot device is just as inappropriate as treating him or her as a real person. The Welsh Captain, for example, appears only briefly, his primary function to provide a choric commentary on Richard's waning support (Act 2 Scene 4), but even he is given some dramatic individuality as he fearfully recalls the menacing omens he has seen.

When you write about characters in *King Richard II* you should therefore try to achieve a balance between analysing their personality, identifying the dilemmas they face, and placing them in their social, critical and dramatic contexts. That style of writing is found all through this Guide, and that, together with the essay example given above (pages 115–18) and the following brief discussions of the major characters will help you with your own written responses.

### King Richard

Shakespeare very much manipulates his audience's response to Richard in his journey from absolute monarch to solitary prisoner.

The king's opening image of confident majesty is progressively undermined by accusations of murder and incompetent government, culminating in his disastrous decision to confiscate Bullingbrook's inheritance. Richard departs for Ireland leaving behind a deeply unhappy group of nobles.

When Richard returns to the stage, Shakespeare has already prepared the ground for his inevitable defeat. Yet as the tyrant king learns of the evaporation of his military and political support, Shakespeare presents him in a new and more sympathetic light. He becomes now a man facing defeat and failure. But not just any man, for Shakespeare's Richard has an ability to study himself from the outside and a special way with words by which he expresses his acute awareness of the transience of worldly glory and the hollowness of kingship. His friends urge him to 'manly' courage and resistance, but Richard, caught up poet-like in his own tragedy, seems impotent, a strangely weak 'feminine' king of tears, emotion and passivity. The once heartless tyrant becomes suddenly aware of his own vulnerability: 'I live with bread like you, feel want, / Taste grief, need friends.'

As Bullingbrook moves inexorably to confront Richard, the king seems paralysed, alternating between a yearning to be freed from the cares of state and a desire to remain centre stage. Yet in the deposition scene, Richard's 'linguistic resistance' manages to turn military defeat into moral victory as he seizes on every dramatic opportunity to highlight the enormity of his 'un-kinging'.

Only when he is alone in prison and reduced to 'nothing' does Richard, born to command, finally fully understand himself. Mankind can never truly be content. Only death can bring release from the cares of this world. Instead of vainly seeking selfish happiness, Richard should instead have looked to serve his country's needs: 'I wasted time and now doth time waste me'.

## Bullingbrook

Henry Bullingbrook (both Holinshed and Shakespeare spell his name this way; the more modern variant is 'Bolingbroke') is in many respects Richard's mighty opposite. He is a member of a military caste, whose profession is war and whose prime concern is to protect itself from the power of an overmighty monarch. But where Richard is articulate and self-revealing, Bullingbrook's stirring rhetoric hides as much as it reveals, so that the audience is forced increasingly to wonder whether his secret ambition is the crown itself.

Initially, Bullingbrook poses as defender of the royal family, seeking revenge for the murder of his uncle, but he is temporarily outmanoeuvred by the king and forced into banishment. When Richard's seizure of Gaunt's lands presents him with the pretext to return, he becomes spokesman of the entire aristocratic establishment as he angrily demands his rightful inheritance. Where Richard had delayed and despaired, Bullingbrook moves with speed and efficiency. Does he secretly desire the crown? Even when the king at Flint Castle hints that his realm is at his cousin's mercy, Bullingbrook is careful to insist that he has no such intention.

Yet, in the very next scene, Bullingbrook formally accepts the crown from Richard and, once king, deals effectively with a dangerous conspiracy, retains the support of York and his family and crushes the last remnants of pro-Richard support. The play finishes with this apparently able and successful king already weighed down with guilt and seeking to do penance by making a pilgrimage to the Holy Land. The audience is left wondering if Richard's murder will haunt Henry's reign just as Gloucester's murder haunted Richard.

### Gaunt, York and Northumberland

All three great magnates share the aristocrats' hostility to Richard's autocratic style of government but each responds to the threat to their baronial class in different ways. Gaunt remains reluctantly loyal to the crown, but unhesitating in his criticism of Richard's actions. His patriotic speech (Act 2 Scene 1) is a lament for the passing of a golden age, where king and nobles were a 'happy breed of men' bound together in 'fealty' (mutual loyalty and obligation), fighting against a foreign enemy. Richard tests Gaunt's loyalty to the limit, yet Gaunt remains to the end a defender of the king's divine right to rule, despite Richard's involvement in Gloucester's murder and his own son's banishment.

York also believes Richard ordered Gloucester's murder, disapproves of the king's policies and nostalgically recalls the great military campaigns of Edward III and the Black Prince, Richard's famous father. When the king seizes Gaunt's lands, York is predictably horrified, for such an act broke the social contract between monarch and noble underpinning the feudal system. Richard may demand complete obedience, but York knows the king must uphold his subjects' legal rights before any such allegiance can be expected.

When Bullingbrook returns to claim his inheritance, York is the embodiment of divided loyalty: how can a man be loyal both to his king and to a kinsman whom the king has wronged? After an agony of indecision York chooses to follow Bullingbrook, only to be confronted with a new dilemma – the discovery of his son's part in the conspiracy to kill the new king at Oxford. Some critics see Shakespeare's York as weak and indecisive, almost comic in his helplessness, but surely there must be some sympathy and respect for a man forced to choose between two irreconcilable allegiances?

Northumberland, in contrast, has no qualms about rebelling. He is from the start an implacable opponent of royal power. The king has acted unjustly against the aristocracy, and must therefore be resisted. Northumberland is very much the Elizabethan machiavel (see page 73), with his manipulation of Ross and Willoughby, his obsequious flattery of Bullingbrook and his disingenuous assurances of loyalty to Richard. There is, however, more than mere scheming villainy to Northumberland, for Shakespeare has him voice very similar concerns about the king's method of government to those of Gaunt and York.

### The king's favourites

King Richard's supporters (Mowbray, Bushy, Green, Bagot, Carlisle and Aumerle) demonstrate in various ways how dangerous late medieval and early modern English politics could be. Mowbray is banished, Bushy and Green are executed, Bagot turns informer to save his own skin and Carlisle is arrested for capital treason. Aumerle first loses his dukedom then almost loses his head for his part in the conspiracy to assassinate King Henry at Oxford.

Mowbray provides a suitably fiery and warlike opponent for Bullingbrook in the opening confrontation and the Trial by Combat. The play strongly hints that Richard gave the order for the Duke of Gloucester's murder (Act 1 Scene 2, lines 4–6) and that Mowbray was in some way involved (see page 5). There is therefore justifiably a hurt dignity in Mowbray's reproach to Richard that he deserved better than 'to be cast forth in the common air'. His bitter regret at never more being able to speak his native tongue is the play's earliest reflection on the importance of language (see pages 12 and 82–3). In keeping with

Shakespeare's balanced presentation on the characters, Carlisle later informs the audience that Mowbray had died in Venice after fighting bravely and honourably for Christ against 'black pagans, Turks and Saracens'. In fact, although the historical Mowbray went on a pilgrimage to the Holy Land, he did not fight there. The Crusades had ended more than a century before.

Bushy, Green and Bagot are examples of the 'Base men . . . made great' by Bullingbrook's confiscated lands (i.e. members of the lower aristocracy recruited to Richard's cause with promises of advancement). Bullingbrook angrily describes them as the 'caterpillars of the commonwealth' whom he has 'sworn to weed and pluck away' (Act 2 Scene 3, lines 165–6) and gives as one of the reasons for executing Bushy and Green the fact that they had benefited from his lost inheritance (Act 3 Scene 1, lines 22–7). There is little to differentiate them in the script, although some productions have been quite inventive: Green could be portrayed as the busy bureaucrat 'caterpillar' who prompts Richard to attend to affairs of state (Act 1 Scene 4, lines 37–41) and who, on hearing news of Bullingbrook's invasion, attempts to stop the king from sailing for Ireland. Bushy might be characterised as the smooth-talking 'caterpillar' who tries to console the queen by use of the 'shifting perspectives' conceit so symbolic of the play's overall structure (Act 2 Scene 2, lines 1–27). Both men, however, remain admirably loyal to Richard and go to their death with dignity, unlike Bagot, the turncoat 'caterpillar', who attempts to incriminate Aumerle in the murder of Gloucester (Act 4 Scene 1, lines 1–19).

The Bishop of Carlisle, first seen with Richard on his return from Ireland, is similarly lightly sketched. His function is primarily to deliver the impressive speech of protest when Bullingbrook attempts to 'ascend the regal throne' (Act 4 Scene 1, lines 114–49), a brave if solitary show of loyalty, for which the bishop is immediately arrested. Again, actors have been imaginative in fleshing out this character. One production assumed a history of deep animosity between Carlisle and Northumberland, which imparted a particular venom to the latter's reaction on learning that an unidentified clergyman was with Richard: 'Oh, belike it is the Bishop of Carlisle' (Act 3 Scene 3, line 30).

The character of the Duke of Aumerle, York's son, is the most developed of all Richard's favourites. Aumerle had received his dukedom from his cousin Richard after Gloucester's death, along with most of his murdered uncle's property. His animosity towards his other cousin, Bullingbrook, is clear from the start of the play when he sarcastically describes the tears he had seemed to weep at Bullingbrook's departure into banishment (Act 1 Scene 4, lines 6–9). Aumerle remains King Richard's loyal companion to the bitter end, however, constantly urging the king to action (Act 3 Scene 2, lines 186–7) and weeping at his distress (Act 3 Scene 3, line 160). Richard's fall from power inevitably leaves Aumerle vulnerable to attack from other ambitious nobles, as the various accusations and challenges to mortal combat demonstrate (Act 4 Scene 1, lines 1–90). Although Bullingbrook defers the Trials by Combat, Aumerle is deprived of his dukedom and his father is required to act as pledge for his son's 'lasting fealty [loyalty] to the new-made king' (Act 5 Scene 2, line 45).

The scenes where York and his wife discover their son's involvement in the Oxford conspiracy show Aumerle in a new, more equivocal light. Is his continuing loyalty to Richard to be admired, or should the audience deplore his cowardly betrayal of the other conspirators? To highlight this mixture of the admirable and the craven in Aumerle's character, one production cast him as a young man scarcely out of his teens: fiercely loyal to Richard, but out of his depth when faced with challenges from battle-hardened knights and easily cowed by an enraged father and a determined mother.

### The female characters

The women in the play are all very much Shakespeare's own invention. The Duchesses of Gloucester and York are scarcely mentioned in Holinshed, Shakespeare's major historical source for his play, while Richard's queen was only a child of ten at the time of his deposition. Some modern critics have suggested that Shakespeare's portrayal of these essentially powerless and marginalised female characters reflects his sympathetic understanding of the inevitable plight of all women in a feudal, male, militaristic world. The function of the women characters in the play, and how they might be seen to challenge rather than reinforce the play's masculine, military values, is discussed more fully in the Contexts section (pages 74–5) and Critical Approaches section (pages 97–9).

### The Gardener

At the heart of the play, between the events at Flint Castle and

Richard's formal deposition, Shakespeare has placed the garden scene (Act 3 Scene 4): a quietly formal and symbolic scene, unlike any other in the play, which brings a brief pause to the seemingly inevitable march of history and allows ordinary working people to give their verdict on events.

As the Gardener sets his assistants to work, he seems in his humble way to be like a mighty prince tending his realm, employing all his gardening statecraft to keep his little country in good order. The Gardener's judgement of Richard's stewardship of England is brutally frank. The queen may believe her husband's deposition to be like Adam and Eve's tragic expulsion from the Garden of Eden, but the Gardener takes a different view. He believes that Richard lost his crown through 'waste of idle hours' and failure to work hard enough at nurturing and controlling his people. Actors have sometimes played the roles of the Gardener and his assistants as comic rustics, which perhaps detracts from the seriousness of their political commentary. John Barton's 1973 production (see page 101) cast them as monks: intelligent and thoughtful men whose vocation would also require them to do humble manual work.

# Resources

## Books

**Richard D Altick**, 'Symphonic Imagery in *Richard II*', in Nicholas Brooke (ed.), *Shakespeare: Richard II*, Casebook series, Palgrave, 1973
A thought-provoking study of the repeated image-themes in *King Richard II*.

**Linda Bamber**, 'History, Tragedy, Gender', in Graham Holderness (ed.), *Shakespeare's History Plays: Richard II to Henry V*, Macmillan, 1992
A feminist reading which sees 'femininity' and 'history' in *King Richard II* as two mutually incompatible contraries.

**Catherine Belsey**, 'Making Histories', in Graham Holderness (ed.), *Shakespeare's History Plays: Richard II to Henry V*, Macmillan, 1992
A study which focuses on the relationship between language and power in *King Richard II*.

**Nicholas Brooke** (ed.), *Shakespeare: Richard II*, Casebook series, Palgrave, 1973
A selection of traditional criticism of *King Richard II* from 1680 to 1970. Includes criticism by Altick, Tillyard, Kantorowicz, Mahood and Rossiter noted in this book list.

**James L Calderwood**, '*Richard II*: Metadrama and the Fall of Speech', in Graham Holderness (ed.), *Shakespeare's History Plays: Richard II to Henry V*, Macmillan, 1992
A demanding postmodern reading centred on language, which sees *King Richard II* as a struggle between Richard's 'sacramental' language and Bullingbrook's 'utilitarian' speech.

**Linda Cookson** and **Bryan Loughrey** (eds.), *Critical Essays on Richard II*, Longman Literature Guides series, Longman, 1989
A wide-ranging collection of essays aimed at a student audience, with useful 'afterthoughts' to promote further thinking about the play.

**Martin Coyle** (ed.), *Shakespeare: Richard II*, Icon Critical Guides, Icon Books, 1998
A very helpful selection of critical writing on *King Richard II*, including radical new readings of the play by more recent critics.

**Terry Eagleton**, *William Shakespeare*, Basil Blackwell, 1986
An example of the postmodern (or deconstructive) approach to

Shakespeare's plays. A short section on *Richard II*, focusing on language, shows how difficult it is to ignore the play's realpolitik: 'only by translating unpleasant political realities into decorative verbal fictions can (Richard) engage with them'.

**Charles R Forker**, *Shakespeare: The Critical Tradition. Richard II*, The Athlone Press, 1998
A comprehensive account of criticism of the play from 1780 to 1920. There is a very detailed bibliography, and Forker's substantial introduction also provides an excellent summary of critical developments throughout the twentieth century.

**Margaret Healy**, *Richard II*, Writers and Their Work series, Northcote House in association with the British Council, 1998
An excellent overview of the play which considers the play's politically subversive nature, gender perspectives, performance interpretations and modern critical readings.

**Graham Holderness** (ed.), *Shakespeare's History Plays: Richard II to Henry V*, New Casebooks series, Macmillan, 1992
A collection of recent criticism of the history plays. Includes criticism by Linda Bamber, Catherine Belsey, James Calderwood, Coppelia Kahn and Robert Ornstein noted in this book list.

**Graham Holderness**, *Shakespeare: The Histories*, Macmillan, 2000
A challenging book that exemplifies a political approach to Shakespeare grounded in the context of his time.

**Graham Holderness**, *Shakespeare: Richard II*, Penguin Critical Guides, Penguin Books, 1989
Provides an excellent introduction to the play that combines politics with historical context.

**Jean E Howard** and **Phyllis Rackin**, *Engendering a Nation*, Routledge, 1997
A feminist reading of the history plays which includes an analysis of the concepts of 'masculinity' and 'femininity' in *Richard II*.

**Coppelia Kahn**, 'The Shadow of the Male', in Graham Holderness (ed.), *Shakespeare's History Plays: Richard II to Henry V*, Macmillan, 1992
A study of the patriarchal world of the play, which sees Richard's predicament as a crisis of masculine identity.

**Ernst H Kantorowicz**, *The King's Two Bodies: A Study in Medieval Political Theology*, Princeton University Press, 1957
Written by a historian, the chapter on *King Richard II* has been highly influential. Reprinted in Nicholas Brooke (ed.), *Shakespeare: Richard II*, Casebook series, Palgrave, 1973.

**Jan Kott**, *Shakespeare Our Contemporary*, Methuen, 1965
An influential, but now much criticised political reading of Shakespeare's plays, which argues that in the history plays each king 'drags behind him a long chain of crimes', and that history is a 'Grand Mechanism', a great staircase of 'murder, perfidy, treachery'.

**M M Mahood**, *Shakespeare's Wordplay*, Methuen, 1957
Her chapter on *King Richard II* is a much admired close study of the play's language and imagery. Reprinted in Nicholas Brooke (ed.), *Shakespeare: Richard II*, Casebook series, Palgrave, 1973.

**C W R D Moseley**, *Shakespeare's History Plays: Richard II to Henry V: The Making of a King*, Penguin Critical Studies series, Penguin Books, 1988
Provides a helpful background to the history plays and includes a detailed commentary on *Richard II*.

**Robert Ornstein**, *A Kingdom for a Stage: The Achievement of Shakespeare's History Plays*, Cambridge, Mass., 1972 (extract in Holderness (ed.), *Shakespeare's History Plays: Richard II to Henry V*, New Casebooks series, Macmillan, 1992)
Challenges Tillyard's assertion that *King Richard II* is essentially supportive of the Tudor status quo, arguing instead that it is about rebellion and the 'universality of contention and change'.

**A P Rossiter**, *Angel with Horns*, Longman, 1961
His essay 'Unconformity in Richard II' challenges Tillyard's interpretation, seeing the play as having a much more complex and ambiguous set of meanings. Reprinted in Nicholas Brooke (ed.), *Shakespeare: Richard II*, Casebook series, Palgrave, 1973.

**Margaret Shewring**, *King Richard II*, Shakespeare in Performance series, Manchester University Press, 1996
A very helpful study of *King Richard II* in performance, from Elizabethan times to the present day.

**Caroline Spurgeon**, *Shakespeare's Imagery and What It Tells Us*, Cambridge University Press, 1935
The first major study of imagery in the plays. Although much criticised today, Spurgeon's identification of image-clusters as a dominant feature of the plays has influenced later studies.

**E M W Tillyard**, *Shakespeare's History Plays*, Chatto and Windus, 1944 (reprinted by Penguin Books, 1991)
Very influential in its day and the standard orthodox interpretation of the history plays, arguing that *King Richard II* is essentially supportive of the Tudor status quo. Has since been challenged by more recent critics (see above).

# Films and audio books

Despite being a popular choice for the stage, there are relatively few film or TV versions of *King Richard II*. The following versions are the most accessible:

*King Richard II* (UK, 1978) Director: David Giles. Derek Jacobi (King Richard).

*King Richard II* (UK, 1989) Director: Michael Bogdanov. Michael Pennington (King Richard).

*King Richard II* (UK, 1995) Director: Deborah Warner. Fiona Shaw (King Richard).

*King Richard II* (UK, 2003) Director: Tim Carroll. Mark Rylance (King Richard).

Versions of the play are available on audio books in the series by Naxos, Arkangel and BBC Radio Collection.

## *King Richard II* on the Web

If you type 'King Richard II Shakespeare' into your search engine, it may find over 234,000 items. Because websites are of wildly varying quality, rapidly disappear or are created, no recommendations can safely be made. But if you have time to browse, you may find much of interest.